The Theory, Not the Theorist

The Case of Karl Marx

Rodger Beehler

UNIVERSITY PRESS OF AMERICA,® INC.
Lanham • Boulder • New York • Toronto • Oxford

Copyright © 2006 by
University Press of America,® Inc.
4501 Forbes Boulevard
Suite 200
Lanham, Maryland 20706
UPA Acquisitions Department (301) 459-3366

PO Box 317
Oxford
OX2 9RU, UK

All rights reserved
Printed in the United States of America
British Library Cataloging in Publication Information Available

Library of Congress Control Number: 2006920424
ISBN-13: 978-0-7618-3403-8 (paperback : alk. paper)

∞™ The paper used in this publication meets the minimum
requirements of American National Standard for Information
Sciences—Permanence of Paper for Printed Library Materials,
ANSI Z39.48—1992

To my friends (including my seven siblings),
who made the journey worth it;
and, especially, to Kai, without whose urging
these pages would never have seen
the public light of day.

"Philosophy unties knots in our thinking, but to do so it must make movements which are as complicated as those knots."

Ludwig Wittgenstein

Contents

Preface		vii
1	Functional Explanation and History	1
2	Productive Activity and Social Forms	31
3	The Theory, Not The Theorist: The Case of Marx	73
4	Marx's Explanation of Historical Change	118
5	Reading Marx	143
Notes		155

Preface

This book seeks to recover Karl Marx's social thought from the uncongenial embrace of 'Marxism'. It does so by establishing (1) that the explanation of historical change implicit in Karl Marx's historical investigations of feudalism, capitalism, and European imperialism is not the 'historical materialist' theory of history which he frequently declared himself to have discovered; (2) that the two types of explanation are flatly contradictory; and (3) that this fact reveals Marx's actual (and largely unread) historical investigations to be a deeply prescient understanding of European history and politics having a compelling relevance to today's world of globalized economies, imperialist politics, and eroding domestic liberties and livelihoods.

Throughout I shall mean by 'Marxism' what is commonly referred to as 'historical materialism'. Historical materialism is a theory of historical change, and the content of that theory is set out fully in Chapter One. In setting it out I draw closely upon the work of G. A. Cohen, who is unquestionably the most lucid and resourceful expositor of historical materialism, and a consistent champion (with many others) of the view that Marx's theory of social change is historical materialism and that historical materialism is the ineliminable core of 'Marxism'. In Chapters One to Three of the book I offer a refutation of 'Marxism' so understood.

I present that refutation in three stages. After setting out fully the central claims of historical materialism, I first engage the progressive, developmental component of the theory. This is its allegation that there is, throughout the course of human history, an autonomous fulfilled tendency toward growth of utilized human productive capacity leading through a succession of social forms to a condition of communal ownership of means of production and an egalitarian distribution of social burdens and rewards. It has been repeatedly argued by G. A. Cohen (for one) that the central explanations which historical materialism gives of social change and of certain key social structural relations within any society are (and must be) functional explanations. I argue that the progressive developmental component of historical materialism cannot be accounted for in this way. Specifically, I show that historical materialism entails claims about the emergence (as distinct from the persistence) of economic and other features of successive social forms that functional explanation cannot account for. This leaves the theory without a tenable explanation of the alleged developmental trend.

In Chapter Two I engage a corollary claim of historical materialism: that (as G. A. Cohen phrases it) the course of social change lies in facts which are in an important sense *a*social. I seek to show that (among other difficulties attaching to this claim) the primary importance assigned by historical materialism to technical knowledge and economic enterprise contravenes this asocial requirement, for the reason that concepts, beliefs, and relationships that are social in the stipulated sense are crucial determinants of the type and mode of application of technical knowledge and the perception of economic opportunity extant in human societies.

In Chapter Three I proceed to address the question whether the explanations Karl Marx himself gives of specific historical instances of social change are of the kind required by 'historical materialism'. I treat of this issue in two stages. In Chapter Three I commence to argue that Marx's explanations are most often not historical materialist explanations, and that one reason why this has not been recognized is because readers have been inclined to rely on Marx as the surest interpreter of his own theory. In fact, Marx is a poor guide to his theory. If we distinguish (as it is important always to do) between the theory a writer's investigations do establish, and the theory a writer thinks and declares his investigations to establish, the theory Marx frequently alleged his researches to establish is not what they do establish, nor is it the theory he himself characteristically employs when explaining in detail actual instances of social change. With Marx, as with any theorist, we must always distinguish between his pronouncements about his theory (which are as fallible as anybody else's) and the theory identifiable in his writings when he is employing rather than talking about the understanding of social change got from his researches.

It is worth remembering that some of Marx's most famous pronouncements about his theory of historical change pre-date, by years, much of the painstaking empirical research and writing that culminated in *Capital*. Nor is it unintelligible that a onetime passionate student of Hegel's social theory, who conceived as a young man a long-term project of investigation directed toward establishing a certain theoretical outcome in deliberate opposition to Hegel, should be vulnerable to continuing to perceive and represent his investigations, both to himself and to others, as having established just that intended outcome, even when they do not do so. But more on this later.

In Chapter Four I continue my argument that Marx's most characteristic explanations of social change are not of the historical materialist type by attending carefully to the account Marx gives of the transition from feudalism to capitalism in Britain. I seek to show that this account violates in a number of ways the dicta of historical materialism. In particular, I argue that Marx explains the demise both of feudalism and capitalism by appeal to a self-transforming dynamic internal to each which generates internal contradictions destructive of the integrity of each form. At the same time, I show that Marx, in explaining the development of feudalism into capitalism, assigns causal status to a great many external as well as indigenous events and circumstances, all of them contingent, and no one of them a sufficient cause of the large scale developments he is describing and explaining. For example, he appeals to such various contingent factors as the development of trade in commodities between European societies, colonial predations by European societies against Africa, Asia, and the Americas, the manner in which markets in one society provoked economic changes in other societies, and so on. This, I show, is entirely to be expected, since if feudalism had an internal dynamic that continually weakened it and made it tend steadily toward decline, that dynamic can, at most, explain that decline. It cannot by itself explain why feudalism was succeeded by capitalism. The explanation of why a specific social form declines is logically distinct from the explanation of why what follows it has the features it has. Very often, the two explanations are empirically distinct as well.

In Chapter Five I attempt briefly to establish the continued claim Marx's writings have on the attention of anyone who seeks to understand and appraise the contemporary human condition. In arguing this I touch upon Marx's treatment of oppression and property, political economy and culture, religion and ideology, freedom and democracy, technology and social change, and justice and community. These themes are abiding (though not always explicitly announced) preoccupations of Marx, and form convenient nodes around which to shape a consideration of the legacy of his writings. At the same time I note, in the course of the chapter, some of the errors and blind alleys that Marx's writings (and their engagement by others) should counsel us to avoid.

I conclude with a word on a feature of the book that may require explanation. Throughout I quote frequently from Marx's writings, sometimes at length. I also quote frequently from G.A. Cohen's writings in Chapters One to Three. I do so deliberately because I think it important that the reader have directly before him or her the position that I am criticizing, in a formulation as accurate as I can make it. Often quotation alone can accomplish this authoritatively. The mistake that has put a theory wrong is frequently tied inextricably to the formulation by the theorist of the problem or putative explanation, and cannot be exhibited convincingly by paraphrase. Relevant quotation also makes the book as self-contained as can be done, and able to be followed by readers not closely acquainted with Marx's writing.

I wish to thank Patrick Grant for reading Chapters One to Four in typescript and identifying an occasional un-planed edge in the expression. I also thank Robert Young of *Apple Photo & Imaging,* Salt Spring Island, for transforming an erratic scan into legible text, and Sheryl Taylor-Munro for her assistance in reading the proofs.

I am indebted to the Social Sciences and Humanities Research Council of Canada for a Research Leave Fellowship in the autumn of 1983, and to the University of Victoria for research leave in the spring of 1987 and the autumn of 1990. Without that support the writing of the book would have been much longer being accomplished.

R.B.

The Pacific Coast
Spring 2005

Chapter One

Functional Explanation and History

As stated in the Preface, I shall throughout mean by 'historical materialism' what G.A. Cohen represents as historical materialism in his two important books *Karl Marx's Theory of History: A Defence* (1978) and *History, Labour, and Freedom* (1988).[1] I shall rely primarily upon the later work, since there Cohen refines and revises in certain ways the formulation of historical materialism set out in the earlier book.

1

In *History, Labour, and Freedom* (hereafter *HLF*) Cohen defines historical materialism as:

> the thesis that there is, throughout history's course, a tendency towards growth of human productive power, and that forms of society (or economic structures) rise and fall when and because they enable or promote, or frustrate or impede, that growth. Human productive activity increases in potency as history unfolds, and social forms accommodate themselves to that material growth process. They flourish to the extent that they help to raise the level of development of the productive forces, and they decline when they no longer do so. (155)

Historical materialism (hereafter HM) is, as this definition makes clear, a thesis about how and why one type of social form is succeeded by another type of social form throughout the course of human history. The explanation is held to lie in a tendency within human societies for productive power to grow. By growth in human productive power is meant increase in the *utilized* capacity available to human beings for the production of those objects or services needed to satisfy the needs of all members of the society (whether or not what is in fact produced goes to meet the needs of all).

Growth of productive power is by HM frequently equated (as in the quoted passage) with growth in the level of development of productive forces, where productive forces "are those facilities and devices which are used to productive effect in the process of production", including not only raw materials and tools or premises but especially human "skills" and "technical knowledge" (*HLF* 4). There is, however, an important ambiguity in talk of the level of development of the productive forces that requires comment. The word 'development' suggests that the growth in question consists of qualitative transformation of the type of productive forces available, one type or types being succeeded (or at least added to) by another type or types. At the same time, expositors of historical materialism (among them Cohen) frequently aver that there is also growth of productive capacity where there is only quantitative increase of existing productive forces. On this latter construal of development, extending the area of cultivated land or increasing the number of hours worked each day by producers comprises growth of human productive power, as much as invention of more efficient tools or development of higher yielding seed. For the moment I shall accept this conjoint way of construing growth. But, as we shall see, the merely quantitative way of interpreting growth of productive power is not sufficient for historical materialism. The theory needs periodic qualitative transformation of productive forces to make even plausible its allegation that growth of productive power drives "epochal" social change.

It bears emphasizing that HM asserts that the tendency of the productive forces to develop is an autonomous tendency, just in the sense that it is held to be independent of the "social forms" or "structures" of human societies (*HLF* 83–4 and *passim*). According to the theory, it is not social structures that explain the tendency of the productive forces to develop. It is that tendency, allegedly rooted "in fundamental material [i.e., non-social] facts of human nature and the human situation" that explains "the rise and fall" of social structures (*HLF* 84) Paramount among the institutional arrangements constituting a society is "the economic structure" of a society, which is held to define the type of "social form" a society is. (Note Cohen's equation in the definition quoted above of "forms of society" with "economic structures".) The features of economic structures, according to HM, are determined by their function, which is to promote development of the productive forces. The specific content of any economic structure (often termed the production relations of a society) is caused to be what it is by the level of development of the forces, which the structure must be functional for the development of. That which has the function of promoting development of the forces is itself a function of the forces to be developed. (In a formulation to which we shall return, "forces select structures according to their capacity to promote development" *Karl Marx's Theory of History* (hereafter *KMTH*, 162.)

The next most basic social relations of a society identified by the theory are those constituting its "political and legal superstructure", whose alleged function is to stabilize the economic structure of the society, and whose features, in turn, are held to be explained by (i.e., to be a function of) the type of economic structure obtaining.

In short, HM asserts that the tendency of the productive forces to develop causes to exist successive economic structures, each of which functions to promote that development, and these successive economic structures cause to exist successive political and legal superstructures that function to stabilize each succeeding economic structure. Furthermore, HM asserts that any other features of a society that have propitious effects on the growth of productive power are also caused to exist because of that propitious functional effect.

It will be now be clear that it is a fundamental tenet of HM that (as Cohen states the matter) "the course of social change lies in facts which are in an important sense *a*social" *(HLF* 83). According to HM, the explanation of why and how social change occurs is not to be traced to social forms themselves, but to something ontologically prior to and independent of social forms. It is this "asocial" something that explains the *type,* and *succession,* of social forms observable in history.

The above summary of HM may usefully be condensed into four theses. (All four formulations follow closely G. A. Cohen—see *HLF* 84, 175–6, and *passim.* Titles of the first and third theses are Cohen's; those of the second and fourth theses are my suggestion.)

1. *The Development Thesis*: There is an autonomous tendency for utilized human productive capacity to develop throughout history.
2. *The Determination Thesis*: This autonomous tendency of utilized human productive capacity to develop throughout history causes human social structures to be so shaped and selected as to allow for and promote that development.
3. *The Primacy Thesis*: The most basic structural relations of a human society are its production relations, or economic structure, whose nature is explained by the level of development of the society's productive capacity, and which economic structure explains, in turn, the nature of the society's legal and political superstructure.
4. *The Subordination Thesis*: In the same way that a society's economic structure explains the type of its legal and political relations, the features of any other non-economic phenomena (including such 'spiritual' phenomena as

religion and nationalism) that have propitious economic effects are also explained by these features being functional for material development.

We have here four levels of functional explanation. (1) Growth in human productive capacity is explained by its being functional for human need satisfaction. (2) Production relations are explained by their being functional for development of productive forces. (3) Legal and political relations are explained by their being functional for production relations. (4) Features of any other non-economic phenomena that contribute to productive growth are explained by their being functional for material development (often through their being functional for something else that is directly functional for material development). As Cohen has expressly stated: "the main explanatory theses of historical materialism are functional explanations" (*HLF* 7).

2

In stating the last of the four theses summarizing HM above, I have drawn upon a revision made by G.A. Cohen in his account of historical materialism in *History, Labour, and Freedom*. In that book Cohen distinguishes between two ways of understanding HM. The theory may be interpreted as asserting that the tendency towards "systematic growth of human productive power" comprises "the centre of historical development", in the sense that any "major" developments in other areas of social life are basically ("in their large lines") explained by that tendency (*HLF* 158–9). Or, HM may be interpreted as asserting only that all important developments in other (non-economic) areas of social life are subject to the autonomous tendency of human productive power systematically to grow, just in that they cannot disrupt it, and they do not contribute to it in any way that diminishes the autonomy of that growth of productive power (159). Cohen denotes the first of these readings of HM as "inclusive" and the second as "restrictive", and he summarizes the difference between the two in this way:

> In inclusive historical materialism material and economic development explains the principal features of other, non-economic or spiritual developments. But restricted historical materialism says of spiritual phenomena [for example, religious or nationalist movements] only that they do not govern material development, and it commits itself to materialist explanation of spiritual phenomena only when, were they not so explained, they would be seen to control material development. (175–6)

Cohen argues for the superiority of a restricted over an inclusive reading of historical materialism by considering as illustration the Protestant Reformation, a major religious development that most historians accept "had extensive economic effects" (*HLF* 176). Because the Reformation had extensive economic effects it provokes the question "which features of non-economic phenomena historical materialism is committed to explaining" (176). Inclusive historical materialism must hold that this religious development, which had extensive economic effects, was itself caused by material and economic developments. If, on investigating the historical evidence, we should find that the Reformation "lacked economic causes" while having extensive economic effects, this would argue against the truth of historical materialism construed as inclusive. However, such a finding would constitute no bar to historical materialism construed as "restricted", provided that what explains the Reformation's having had these economic consequences is that "the features of Protestantism *in virtue of which it had* economic effects *arose because of* their tendency to have such effects" (176, my italics).

Throughout this and subsequent chapters I shall take HM to mean (unless otherwise indicated) what Cohen terms restricted historical materialism. Note that restricted as much as inclusive historical materialism is committed to functional explanation. While restricted historical materialism has only to produce a "materialist explanation" of those features of non-economic phenomena that have economic effects, "the appropriate way of explaining such features", Cohen declares, "is by recourse to functional explanation" (*HLF*, 176).

I now turn to a close examination of functional explanation as recruited by HM. I shall seek to show that the use which may be made of functional explanation by 'historical materialists' (or any other social theorist) is more confined than Cohen and others appear to suppose, and that functional explanation cannot do for HM what is expected of it. The appearance that it can will be seen to rest upon ambiguity and error.

3

I begin by distinguishing between the emergence and persistence of social forms. Consider the difference between:

1. Social form S emerged because of cause E.

2. Social form S emerged because of cause C, but it persisted because of cause E

It will immediately be clear that what explains the emergence of a social form need not be what explains its persistence.

Historical materialism is a thesis about the succession of social forms. It affirms that social forms succeed one another according as these forms promote or retard growth of human productive power. As Cohen remarks, "the tendency of history", according to HM, "is progressive": "As history proceeds, increasingly higher levels of productive power are attained, with widely liberating consequences" (*HLF*, 78). Furthermore, HM asserts that the successive social transformations necessary to this progress are (in some sense of this word) "inevitable" (*HLF*, 51–82 and *passim*).

However, once we distinguish between the emergence and the persistence of social forms, it becomes obvious that HM is ambiguous between two quite different claims.

3. Each successive social form emerges, and persists, because it promotes growth of human productive power.

4. Each successive social form may emerge because it promotes growth of human productive power, or it may emerge because of causes unconnected (wholly or in part) to its promoting growth of human productive power, but it persists because it promotes that growth.

What is at issue between these two different claims can be brought out by returning for a moment to the Protestant Reformation. Cohen declares (in a passage some words of which were quoted at the end of the previous section—italics are mine):

> Inclusive historical materialism is challenged *both* by the claim that the Protestant Reformation lacked economic causes *and* by the claim that it had extensive economic effects, whereas restricted historical materialism is challenged by the second claim only. That challenge collapses if the features of Protestantism in virtue of which it had economic effects arose because of their tendency to have such effects. (176)

In this passage two claims are alleged by Cohen to be compatible with restricted historical materialism; that is, with HM as I am interpreting it. (Throughout I shall ignore the definite-description problems attaching to the word 'Protestantism'.)

5. Protestantism was not caused to emerge by economic factors.

6. Those features of Protestantism that had extensive economic effects emerged because of their tendency to have those effects.

There is a tension between these two claims which may be highlighted by stating each more explicitly.

7. The religious convictions and practices constituting 'Protestantism' that arose in Europe in the sixteenth century were not caused to emerge by economic factors.

8. Certain of the religious convictions and practices constituting 'Protestantism' that arose in Europe in the 16th century, were caused to emerge by the fact of their tendency to have certain economic effects.

I submit that claims 7 and 8 are, as they stand, contradictory. Claim 8 attributes to some of the constitutive features of Protestantism certain economic consequences that are said to be the cause of these constitutive features arising. Yet claim 7 denies that any of the constitutive features of Protestantism had economic causes.

One way to seek to overcome the contradiction would be to allege that Protestantism changed from a content it had when it first emerged to a later content (composed of additions to or modifications of the original content), and that it is this later content that was economically propitious. On this construction, 7 and 8 do not contradict one another because the word 'Protestantism' refers to something different in the second of the two claims from what it means in the first. However, a problem with this amendment is that we still have it claimed that some part of what historically comprises 'Protestantism' was caused to occur because of economic factors, while if we return to the first of the two claims addressed by Cohen in the quoted passage we find it asserted that no part of the Protestant Reformation had economic causes. If, on looking at the historical record, we should discover that the economically propitious parts of Protestantism were in fact there from the beginning, or, if we find that, though they were later accretions, they nevertheless comprise constitutive parts of what is termed 'the Protestant Reformation' or 'Protestantism', we still have a contradiction.

There is, however, a different way to avoid a contradiction. This would be to replace statements 5 and 6—and so statements 7 and 8—with the statement:

9. The complex of religious convictions and practices constituting 'Protestantism' arose because of non-economic factors, but certain of Protestantism's features *persisted* because of their tendency to have certain economic effects.

The distinction between the emergence of some entity or feature and the persistence of that entity or feature will, I hope, now be clear. In an epilogue to his chapter "Restricted and Inclusive Historical Materialism" in *HLF,* Cohen comments briefly on why some people are inclined to resist the idea that restricted historical materialism "can qualify as even a construal of historical materialism". The reason, he suggests, is that these persons "have never properly separated, and neither did I in *KMTH*, questions about how the elements within a society are related from questions about how social forms [i.e., types of society] succeed one another" *(HLF,* 178*).* Cohen is right to stress that these different questions must be kept separate. But so, too, must questions about why a feature of a society emerges be kept separate from questions about why a feature of a society persists. With this distinction in mind, let us turn more directly to functional explanation.

4

G.A.Cohen and other expositors of historical materialism frequently assert (or imply) that Charles Darwin's evolutionary theory employs functional explanation, and Cohen himself repeatedly proffers biological examples as instances of phenomena admitting (at least logically) of functional explanation. In *Karl Marx's Theory of History* he discusses species' camouflage, the long tails of cows, petal closure in flowers, and giraffes' long necks.[2]

More recently, in *History, Labour, and Freedom*, he has only introduced the question of functional explanation when he follows it immediately with two examples, the first from biology:

> What is functional explanation? Here are two examples of it: 'Birds have hollow bones because hollow bones facilitate flight', 'Shoe factories operate on a large scale because of the economies large scale brings'. In each case something (birds having hollow bones, shoe factories operating on a large scale) which has a certain effect (flight facilitation, economies of scale) is explained by the fact that it has that effect. (8)

It will be helpful to begin our consideration of HM and functional explanation by examining in detail these two illustrative examples produced by Cohen of functional explanation. I shall attend first to the biological example and then to the factory example. Afterwards I shall return to the Protestant Reformation case touched upon in Section 3 above.

Consider Cohen's first illustrative example of functional explanation:

F1. Birds have hollow bones because hollow bones facilitate flight.

The first thing to notice about F1 is that it is vague as to whether extinct as well as extant species of bird are collected under the assertion. For simplicity's sake, I shall take the assertion to refer only to extant species of bird. Even with this confinement, however, F1 still leaves it unclear which of the following three statements is being asserted:

F2. All extant species of bird have hollow bones because hollow bones facilitate flight.

F3. Those extant species of bird that are capable of flight have hollow bones because hollow bones facilitate flight.

F4. Those extant species of bird that are capable of flight developed hollow bones because hollow bones facilitate flight.

Now HM, recall, is a thesis asserting that social forms evolve over time according as they obstruct or promote growth of human productive power. Suppose I ask which of the above three renderings of F1 is most analogous to the progressive theory of social evolution posited by HM? The answer, clearly, is F4. Yet it should now be obvious that F4 is itself ambiguous between:

F5. In those extant species of bird that are capable of flight, hollow bones emerged because hollow bones facilitate flight.

F6. In those extant species of bird that are capable of flight, hollow bones (once they fortuitously arise in some member or members of the species) persist as a species feature because hollow bones facilitate flight.

If we construe F4 as F5, we have it claimed that what explains hollow bones emerging in certain species of bird is the fact that hollow bones facilitate flight. This claim is false. I can perhaps most helpfully establish its falsehood by shifting for a moment to a related, but defining, characteristic of birds: feathers. Consider the claim:

F7. Those extant species of bird that are capable of flight developed feathers because feathers facilitate flight.

This claim, too, is false. Feathers do facilitate flight. But this effect of feathers neither logically, nor biologically, licenses the conclusion that birds developed feathers because of this effect. It is important to see why this is so.

To the best of our current knowledge, birds evolved from the species Archaeopteryx, itself descended from a type of small dinosaur called coelurosaurs. The prevailing judgment now is that dinosaurs were warm-blooded creatures. Archaeopteryx was feathered, including feathered wings and tail, but the paleontologist John Ostrom, who has examined the five existing fossil specimens of Archaeopteryx, has argued on anatomical grounds that this first bird could not fly, and that its feathers were adaptively favourable for reasons having nothing to do with flight.[3] According to Ostrom, Archaeopteryx's feathered forearms were joined to its shoulder in a way that is anatomically dysfunctional for flapping a wing. In his judgment, feathers had two altogether different functions in the species: insulation to protect against heat loss, and facilitation of the creature's ability to entrap flying insects and other small prey in an enclosed embrace of its feathered forearms. But the insulatory feature is arguably the most important, for the reason that flightless Archaeopteryx was a small animal (about the size of a crow) weighing less than a pound. It had, consequently, a very high ratio of surface area to volume. The relevance of this fact is explained by Stephen Jay Gould:

> Heat is generated over a body's volume and radiated out through its surface. Small warm-blooded creatures have special problems in maintaining a constant body temperature since heat dissipates so quickly from their relatively enormous surface. Shrews, although insulated with a coat of hair, must eat nearly all the time to keep their internal fires burning. The ratio of surface to volume was so low in large dinosaurs that they could maintain constant temperatures without insulation. But as soon as any dinosaur or its descendant became very small, it would need insulation to remain warm-blooded [and survive]. Feathers may have served as a primary adaptation for constant temperatures in small dinosaurs . . .
>
> Feathers, evolved primarily for insulation, were soon [i.e., possibly in a few hundreds of thousands of years] exploited for another purpose in flight. Indeed, it is hard to imagine how feathers could have evolved [i.e., became a species' feature] if they never had a purpose apart from flight. The ancestors of birds were surely flightless, and feathers did not arise all at once and fully formed. How could natural selection build an adaptation through several intermediate stages in ancestors that had no use for it? By postulating a primary function for insulation, we may view feathers as a device for giving warm-blooded dinosaurs an access to the ecological advantages of small size.[4]

In short, without our knowing (and note that Gould says nothing about) what explains the origination of feathers in progenitors of the species Archaeopteryx, there is reason to believe that what explains the persistence of feathers in this early bird is (at least in part) their beneficial effect regarding thermoregulation. Or more briefly:

F8. Feathers were retained by Archaeopteryx because feathers facilitate thermoregulation in small warm-blooded creatures.

But, to repeat, this says nothing about what explains feathers originating in this type of dinosaur. The functional explanation at work in F8 invokes what Darwin termed 'natural selection' (the conferral by specific morphological features of a reproductive advantage in a specific local environment), and as the population geneticist R.C. Lewontin has remarked: "Natural selection of the character states is the essence of Darwinism. All else is molecular biology."[5] That is to say, environmental selection of an already emerged morphological feature that is functional for survival and/or reproduction is no explanation of why or how the morphological feature emerged in the first place.

Returning to hollow bones, what explains the emergence of this skeletal feature involves (as with feathers) genetic phenomena: some mix of mutation, timing shift, gene duplication, or whatever. But whatever the explanation, this fortuitous happy feature eventually conferred an advantage on its possessors in nutritional and reproductive competition because it better enabled these feathered creatures to accomplish flight. Hence, while it is false that birds developed hollow bones because hollow bones facilitate flight, it is true that:

F9. Hollow bones have persisted, in those species of bird capable of flight, in part because hollow bones facilitate flight.

Or, more clearly:

F10. Hollow bones have persisted, in those species of bird capable of flight, in part because hollow bones facilitate flight, thereby better enabling members of these species to survive (and so reproduce).

The point of the words 'in part' in each of F9 and F10 is to register the fact that a part of the explanation of hollow bones persisting in the relevant species is that bone structure is genetically transmitted. Except it were, the mere fact that hollow bones facilitate flight would not result in persistence of the feature in the species. To put it the other way about, we need to appreciate that while some feature's having a certain function may enter into the explanation of some state of affairs, it may not be the whole of the explanation of that state of affairs. Functional relations may form part of the explanation of something, and yet be co-ordinate with (or even subordinate to) other relations and events that are just as much causes (or even more primary causes) of the state of affairs in question.

Where does this leave Cohen's F1 illustrative statement that "Birds *have* hollow bones because hollow bones facilitate flight"? Having found the F4 developmental rendering of F1 to be false, let us construe Cohen's sentence according to the more plausible of the remaining two interpretations:

F3. Those extant species of birds that are capable of flight have hollow bones because hollow bones facilitate flight.

F3 is true, if it asserts:

F11. Hollow bones continue to persist in those extant species of birds that are capable of flight (in part) because hollow bones facilitate flight, thereby better enabling members of these species to survive and so reproduce.

But F2 is false if it asserts:

F12. Hollow bones arose in those extant species of birds that are capable of flight because hollow bones facilitate flight, thereby better enabling members of these species to survive and so reproduce.

Recall Cohen's schematic parsing of his illustrative functional explanation claim F1, "Birds have hollow bones..." (emphases are mine):

Something [birds having hollow bones...] which has a *certain effect* [flight facilitation...] is explained by *the fact that it has* that effect. (*HLF*, 8)

Suppose you and I are observing a particular bird perched on a fencepost, and I ask you 'Why does that bird have hollow bones?' Would the explanation be the singular fact that such bones have the effect of facilitating flight? Where our focus is a particular bird, we shall all (Cohen included) readily agree that to explain why this specific organism has this particular morphological feature involves a great many more facts than that hollow bones facilitate flight. But if we shift our focus to those existing species of birds that are capable of flight, does anything change? If I ask you 'Why do birds have hollow bones?', is the explanation the singular fact that hollow bones facilitate flight?

Compare the question and answer: 'Why are there birds?' — 'Birds are capable of flight.' Everyone will agree that the fact that birds are capable of flight is no explanation of the fact that birds came to exist. Their capacity for flight may enter into the explanation of their continuing to exist. But it is no part of the explanation of their coming into existence.

Yet Cohen in more than one place treats the *functional* relation between a feature and an effect as *explanatory of the feature's occurring*, where by 'occurring' is meant its coming into existence. He repeatedly argues that if the existence of a certain feature would have a certain effect, that dispositional fact explains its occurring (i.e., its coming about).

We find Cohen doing so, for example, in two chapters of *KMTH* in which he treats at length of functional explanation. In that earlier book, too, historical materialism is "presented as a functionalist theory of history and society" (249), and Cohen begins his discussion of functional explanation with six illustrative sentences, three of which we have already encountered above in identical, or virtually identical, form: "Birds have hollow bones because hollow bones facilitate flight". "Shoe factories operate on a large scale because of the economies large scale brings." "Protestantism achieved strength in early modern Europe because it promoted the development of capitalism" (*KMTH*, 249–50). In the course of his discussion, Cohen represents functional explanation as a type of "consequence explanation", and he depicts consequence explanations as having this form:

IF it is the case that if an event of type E were to occur at t_1, then it would bring about an event of type F at t_2, THEN an event of type E occurs at t_3. (*HLF*, 260)

The word 'event' in this schema ranges over the acquisition by an organism of some feature or property, and Cohen gives a more specific formulation for such an event case in the schema:

IF it is true of an object 0 that if it were F at ^{t1}, then it would, as a result, be E at ^{t2}, THEN 0 is F at ^{t3}. (*KMTH*, 261)

As Cohen summarizes the schema, "it is the fact that *were an event of a certain type to occur, it would have a certain effect*, which explains the occurrence of an event of the stated type" (261, Cohen's emphasis).

Note the word 'occurrence' here, and note that it clearly refers to the emergence of the relevant event. The upshot is the position:

IF it is the case that were birds to have hollow bones they would be more capable of flight, THEN this fact explains the emergence of hollow bones in birds.

For reasons already sketched, this claim is false. Its falsehood is connected to its ignoring the difference between enabling conditions and operative causes. It is a condition enabling persons to harm you by a blow to the face that your body have the form and vulnerable properties it has. But those enabling properties are not sufficient to explain someone's so striking and harming you, should they do so. In the same way, it is a condition enabling flight that birds have hollow bones. But that enabling property does not explain hollow bones arising in specific members of the species, which explanation lies (to recall Richard Lewontin's remark) not in *natural selection* but in *molecular biological* processes. Natural selection operates upon *already emerged* enabling properties possessed by individual species's members. It is microbiological processes that *cause* the emergence of such enabling properties in individuals in the first place.

We see Cohen eliding this distinction in the following sentences about evolution in *KMTH* 269:

> Two sorts of consequence generalizations are supported by the fossil record, current observation, and inferences therefrom. In the first, or *diachronic* case [which, Cohen states, alone "provides a genuine explanation"], it is true at a time t that were a species to have a certain feature it would fare better, and true at a later time $t+n$ that the species has the feature. (More precisely, the disposition obtaining at t raises the probability of the truth at $t+n$ the of the antecedent of the hypothetical specifying it.). . . . An illustration of the diachronic case. A population of giraffes with a mean neck length of six feet lives in an environment of acacia trees, on whose leaves they feed. The height of the trees make it true that if they now had longer necks, their survival prospects would be better. They subsequently come to have longer necks. So far all we have is evidence of

a consequence generalization. But if Darwin's theory of evolution is true, then the fact that were they to have had longer necks, they would have fared better, contributes to explaining the elongation. The environment selects in favour of variants with longer necks precisely because it is an environment in which longer necks improve life chances [and so improve reproductive contribution to the species's gene pool].

Cohen's assertion that the fact that longer necks dispose toward improved life chances contributes to explaining the elongation of necks in the species is true, just in the sense that this dispositional fact contributes to explaining the *persistence* of longer necks among the species, *if and when* these arise in individual members. But it is false that the fact that longer necks dispose toward improved life chances contributes to explaining the emergence of longer necks in the first place. The dispositional fact contributes to explaining the elongation only in the sense that *except* that dispositional fact held, the appearance of longer necks in specific members of the population would have no evolutionary consequence. But that dispositional fact does not itself cause the appearance of longer necks in specific members. As Cohen's own last quoted sentence states, the environment "selects in favour of variants *with longer necks*"—i.e., it selects in favour of individuals *in whom* (as a result of whatever genetic causes) a longer neck *has emerged*. That longer necks are favoured by the environment does not cause longer necks to emerge in individuals (to be then favourably selected).

In other words, while the dispositional fact in question does form part of the explanation of the elongation of the species's neck length over time, it does not form part of the operative causes that explain long necks arising. Rather, the dispositional fact forms part of the operative cause of long necks persisting, giving rise in time to longer mean neck length.

Notice that Cohen himself reduces the "diachronic" case to the proposition that the dispositional fact that longer necks improve life chances "raises the *probability*" that longer necks will obtain at $t+n$. This downward modification provokes the question why, if only probability holds in evolutionary theory, *inevitability* allegedly holds in HM (a question we shall take up in detail later). But at this point it is enough to see that Cohen's downward modification complies with the analysis given above. It is true that the fact that a dispositional relation (longer necks improving life chances) which is necessary to a causal process (selection in an extant environment) does obtain (longer necks do improve life chances in the extant environment) raises the probability of the causal process actually taking place. But not everything that increases the probability of a process taking place is sufficient to cause it to take place.

We arrive, then, at the result that the first of Cohen's illustrative examples of functional explanation is deeply problematic. It is important to see the two ways in which it is problematic.

1. The purported functional explanation statement is false in so far as it attributes *emergence* of the feature, hollow bones, to that feature's facilitating flight.

2. The purported functional explanation statement is false in so far as it attributes *persistence* of the feature, hollow bones, *solely* to that feature's facilitating flight.

Finally, it is important to notice that both in the hollow bones and feathers cases, the *effect* in question (facilitating flight) is a potentiality, not an actuality. Hollow bones and feathers facilitate flight. But this fact does not *determine* either that any organism will, in fact, be favoured with these features, or, that an organism so favoured will, in fact, fly. Much else must happen to get from the fact that hollow bones and feathers facilitate flight to the fact that there exists a hollow-boned feathered species whose members do fly. Not least: the animals so constituted must *behave* so as to *exploit* this feature.

5

I turn now to Cohen's second example of functional explanation, 'Shoe factories operate on a large scale because of the economies large scale brings'. It will now be obvious that this sentence leaves unclear whether what is being asserted is one, or both, of the following propositions.

F13. Operation on a large scale arose in shoe factories because of the economies large scale brings.

F14. Operation on a large scale has persisted in shoe factories because of the economies large brings.

It will also, I hope, now be obvious that the truth or falsehood of each of these assertions is independent of the other. Cause of origin and cause of persistence are not only logically, they are very often empirically, distinct. (One need look no farther than the marriages and occupations of human beings for familiar confirmation.)

Let us concentrate on F13, and, more specifically, on the *change* it implies between two states:

State S, at time T1, when shoe factories operated on a small scale.

State L, at time T2, when shoe factories operate on a large scale.

Suppose we denote the changes of scale that distinguish S from L, 'C', and the economies that C produces, 'E'. Cohen's second example of a functional explanation claim, then, asserts (according to the Cohen schema):

F15. Something, C, which has a certain effect E, is *explained* by the fact that it has effect E.

However, this way of stating the matter submerges the feature of the example that is most relevant to historical materialism: that the appeal to functional explanation is supposed to explain *the change* from S to L—why that change does, in fact, take place. To bring out this feature we need to recast the claim as:

F16. Something, C, which has a certain effect E, *comes about* because it has that effect E.

Or more graphically:

F17. If C, then E; therefore, C (comprising L).

Clearly, this will not do (unless one is an Aristotelian). The only way to render the F17 reading of F13 tenable is to read it as a paraphrase of:

F18. Some agent or group of agents appreciates that if C, then E, and accordingly acts to bring about C, and (therefore) E, thus comprising a change from state S to state L.

So much for emergence. Turning to F14—that large scale operation has persisted in shoe factories because of the economies large scale brings—the truth of this claim does not require that some agent or group of agents purposely introduces larger scale because of its appreciated economic effects. Its truth is compatible (as Cohen points out) with some analogue of chance variation and natural selection obtaining, according to which whatever causes larger scale to arise in specific firms, such increased scale confers competitive advantage and/or increased profitability and, consequently, persists because so.

Note, however, that it is implausible to propose that large scale could come to be a *persistent* feature of the shoe *industry* without its being recognized that it does confer economies, and so without its being, henceforth, purposely pursued by all firms. Indeed, given the expenditure in capital and time and the attendant risk that increased scale involves (which increased scale is not to be confused with the exploitative device of simply exacting more work for each day's wages), it is implausible to propose that "chance variation" or "drift" are sufficient to generate significant scale changes at the industry level. It is insistently claimed not only by Marx but by other theorists of capitalist economics (including Max Weber) that most of the micro-activity of an industry that produces macro-effects is explicitly, or intuitively, driven by intelligent provision. Even entrepreneurs who 'fly by the seat of their pants' do so by reference to consciously pursued objectives and roughly conceived criteria of performance, and this is true the more 'micro' the activity in question. Furthermore, scale of operation is one of those variables that a capitalist entrepreneur can most immediately discern changes in. For these reasons, whatever explains introduction of increased scale, persistence of increased scale in specific firms and its consequent translation into an industry feature is not credibly credited to non-intentional activity. One cannot have it both ways. Either a basic feature of capitalist production is that virtually all activities (and claims) falling under its aegis are ruthlessly governed by reference to money, with the result that scale, which carries the obvious possibility of 'over-extension', will be closely overseen; or, this is not a basic feature of capitalism, in which case a good many of Marx's other claims (for which there is much evidential support) become problematic.

Note, further, that where functional explanation is purposive, Cohen's schema is strictly inaccurate. We may see this if we return, first, to the issue of emergence, and the three statements:

F15. Something, C, which has a certain effect E, is explained by the fact that it has that effect.

F16. Something, C, which has a certain effect E, comes about because it has that effect.

F18. Some agent or group of agents appreciates that if C, then E, and accordingly acts to bring about C, and (therefore) E.

Where F18 is the correct explication of F16, then schema F15, as it stands, does not correctly map the situation. Rather, the correct schema must be something like:

F15*. Something, C, which has a certain effect E, is explained by the fact that it *is recognized* by some agent or agents as having that effect E, and produced accordingly.

That is to say, the dispositional fact does not alone explain the occurrence of what was the dispositive effect. The dispositional fact is a part of the explanation of the occurrence of what has that effect. But that does not make it the case that occurrence of what has the dispositive effect (large scale) "is explained by" the dispositional fact that things of this kind have that effect. To this dispositional fact we must add intentional activity on the part of agents cognizant of that dispositional fact.

The same holds for persistence at the industry level, which involves the state of affairs:

F19. Some agent or group of agents appreciates that if C, then E, and accordingly acts to continue (or duplicate) C, and (therefore) E.

Here too, the schema needed to map the situation is a variant of F15*:

F15**. Something, C, which has a certain effect E, is explained by the fact that it is recognized by some agent or agents as having that effect, and continued (or duplicated) accordingly.

Up to this point I have been attempting to show that functional explanation cannot plausibly support the assertion of a tendency for large scale production to become a feature of the shoe industry unless *purposive* functional explanation is invoked. We now need to attend to a different issue provoked by invocation of functional explanation in the shoe industry case—one involving the difference between purposive and non-purposive functional explanation of increasing scale, but which also extends into the whole enterprise of functionally explaining features of economic arrangements.

6

Scale of production can be regarded as a productive force, in that increased scale very often multiplies productivity. Or, it may be regarded as a production relation—a feature of how existing forces are deployed in labouring. (At one time in a society, m forces employed in shoe production may be divided among n productive enterprises; at a later time, the same quantity m of productive forces may be concentrated among n-s productive enterprises, each of which operates on a large scale.) One can find texts in Marx's writings favouring both conceptions. On the second conception, HM asserts that increased scale arises because it facilitates optimal use of existing forces. On the first conception, HM asserts that increased scale arises because it is itself growth of productive forces. Whichever version one chooses, we encounter the allegation that something selects something else. People select increased scale as a further productive force, or, "forces select" increased scale as facilitating their optimal employment.

The expression 'forces select', we have already seen, is Cohen's (from *KMTH* 162). At the place where the expression occurs Cohen further asserts: "The forces develop only within suitable relations, but it is false that whether they develop is settled independently of the forces by the character of the relations, since the forces decide the character of the relations." (162) What I wish briefly to show is that when we probe this "forces select" formulation, we find that it too can only be construed as invoking purposive functional explanation.

Compare the two statements:

ET: Environments select features according to their capacity to promote the survival and reproduction of organisms possessing them.

HMT: Forces select structures according to their capacity to promote development of the forces selecting them.

Notice a disanalogy between the functional explanation statement drawn from evolutionary theory (hereafter ET) and the HM functional explanation statement. According to the HM assertion, that which is to develop selects that which is propitious for its (own) development. But in the ET statement, that which is to develop is not that which selects, but that which is selected. In evolution within nature, the environment is not the locus of development (selecting that which is propitious for its own development). The locus of development is the species bearing the features selected. In evolution of species, that which has developed—a feature of a species' varietal type—is selected by what does not itself develop—the environment. (Actually, this is a simplification; some organisms interact with the environment in such a way as to alter it over very long periods of time, creating a feedback loop with selection. But for the moment, I shall ignore that complexity and treat the simplification as adequate.) In the ET statement, the environment does not select what enables it to develop. It selects what enables the bearers of what is selected to develop. The environment "selects" not what is adaptive *for it*, but what is adaptive to it. In HM, in contrast (whose time frame is miniscule compared to natural selection) the primary locus of development lies in *what does the selecting*, not in what is the bearer of the features selected. What is selected is selected because it is propitious *for what selected it*. This contrasts with natural selection, wherein what is selected is selected because it is propitious for the bearers of what is selected. In other words, whereas in ET functional explanation, the selected property is selected because it benefits the *selectee* (if one may so express it), in HM functional explanation the selected property is selected because it benefits the *selector*.

But this suggests that the only way to construe HM functional explanation is to take it as asserting purposive explanation. That is, the HM functional explanation statement above must be construed as meaning, not literally that "forces select", but rather that:

Human societies select structures according to their capacity to promote development of forces of production.

However, an obvious problem with this construction is that, in it, the ambiguity of emergence and/or persistence reappears. We need now to take account of the full implication for the theory of this ambiguity.

The Development Thesis, recall, asserts that there is an autonomous tendency for utilized human productive capacity to develop throughout history. This progressive thesis cannot amount only to the claim that, wherever, by some happy event, some productive advance does occur, human societies will select that advance. This asserts mere persistence of whatever advances in productive capacity do happen, in fact, to emerge. Nevertheless, a text that Cohen (for one) has repeatedly quoted in exposition of Marx's alleged historical materialism (he quotes it twice in *HLF* and once in *KMTH*)[6] is precisely of this type. The text is some sentences from a letter by Marx to P. V. Annekov, dated 28 December 1846—note the date. (Robert Tucker is another who regards the letter as, in his words, "a trenchant statement of the [historical] materialist conception of history".[7]) Italics are mine.

> Men never relinquish what they *have won*, but this does not mean that they never relinquish the social form in which they *have acquired* certain productive forces. On the contrary, in order that they not be *deprived* of the result *attained* and *forfeit* the fruits of civilization, they are obliged, from the moment their mode of carrying on commerce no longer corresponds to the productive forces acquired, to change all their traditional social forms.[8]

There is not a thing in these sentences that addresses the question of how the fruits in question have emerged. The text is throughout a conditional attribution: if and where such fruits are won, they will not be relinquished. They (allegedly) will be made to persist. But this is not enough to warrant the Development Thesis.

For the Development Thesis, to repeat, affirms a continuous, "*by and large, fulfilled*", tendency for productive power to grow throughout the course of history (*HLF*, 87). This foundational thesis of HM, then, requires that there be continued emergence of new productive capacity, not just continuation of such increased capacity as should happen, or not, to emerge. The question immediately arises: how is HM plausibly to account for the predicated emergence?

One answer to this question would be that human beings, being intelligent, rational, and innovative, and existing in conditions of scarcity, do deliberately (and successfully) pursue increase of productive capacity throughout history. The difficulty with this answer is threefold: it contradicts things Marx frequently says or suggests; it jars with the historical record; and it is inherently implausible, even prior to examining the historical record. G.A. Cohen himself iterates all three of these difficulties when he remarks that "it is false—it could not be true—that the whole of history has a purpose which humanity sets and pursues, and in his more sober moments Marx ridicules just such claims". (*HLF* 150. Note, by the way, the distinction here between Marx "sober" and Marx not sober, to which I shall return in Chapter Three.)

The idea that the Development Thesis posits "individual producers, or co-operating groups of them, striving to upgrade their skills and means of production, so that labour will lie less heavily upon them [and human wants will be more fully as well as more easily satisfied?], a picture in which global productive progress [throughout the course of history] is the aggregate result of those several strivings", is termed by Cohen "the Rational Adaptive Practices", or RAP, view of the Development Thesis. (*HLF* 87–8. The expression is taken from Andrew Levine and Erik Wright.) Historical research reveals that changes in productive forces advancing productive capacity have frequently proceeded not from an intention on the part of anyone to augment productive capacity, but from quite different motivations arising from the situation of persons within the power relations of the society. Cohen accepts this evidence, and proposes a non-RAP account of development. But his proposal, when we examine it, leaves the problem of emergence up in the air. (Emphases are mine).

> The non-RAP claim is not that rational producers introduce superior forces in order to lighten their own labour: that this occurs is not denied, but it is not put forward as the general case. Instead, the claim is that, being rational, people *retain and reject* relations of production according as the latter do and do not allow productive improvement *to continue*. In the singularly apt formulation of Philippe Van Parijs, the non-RAP claim does not posit a 'search-and-selection process which operates directly on the . . . productive forces' but 'one which operates on the relations of production, which in turn control the search-and-selection of productive forces' . . . The tendency [to productive development] is not now seen as an effect of the 'class-specific rationalities' attached to given sets of social relations. On the contrary. Particular class-specific rationalities prevail only as long as they are associated with class structures which serve a more basically grounded impulsion to productive progress. (*HLF* 91. See also 23–24 for a virtually identical passage.)

In the last sentence of this passage we see reiterated the claim that something asocial explains the nature of what is social ("class structures"). But the passage as a whole leaves unanswered how the Development Thesis is to account for the emergence of those forces without which there cannot be productive *progress*. To assert that people retain and reject relations of production according as these allow or obstruct improvement leaves unexplained the *origin* of that which these relations promote or hinder employment *of*. Nor does

Cohen's invocation of Van Parijs's search-and-selection device remove this obscurity. Van Parijs's account alleges search-and-selection that does not operate directly on productive forces, but on production relations. I take this to mean that the rational human choices driving progress engage relations, not forces, while these relations allegedly "in turn control the search-and-selection of productive forces". But what do these last quoted ten words mean? It looks like they must mean that persons search-for and-select forces *from within their production relations roles*, with the attendant class specific rationalities stressed by Levine and Wright. But, to repeat, this renders implausible the positing of a constant "impulsion" to productive advance, for the reason (already noted) that, where class rationalities operate, there is no reason to suppose a constant interest in innovation of forces and much reason to deny it. Ruling classes are, very frequently, most concerned to safeguard or increase their own want satisfactions, and, consequently, often meet the proposal—or fact—of economic change with outright opposition. Exploited classes, on the other hand, are (as the adjective implies) subject to the economic relations constituting the "social form" of the society. To attribute to these persons the locus of continued productive advance is implausible by appeal to HM's own categories.

Cohen effectively admits these difficulties in this passage from the very first chapter of *HLF*:

> In *KMTH* I suggested, rather rashly, that, as long as scarcity prevails, people [note the general term: RB] will tend to take whatever opportunities there are for expanding productive power, since it would be irrational for them not to. I now concede that . . . rationality does not always favour productive innovation, even where it is possible to achieve it. A ruling class in secure control of the productive process might sometimes have good reason not to allow productive innovation and to try to extract more from the immediate producers without improving existing techniques. More generally: since it takes time and energy to introduce innovations, and since the process of introducing them carries opportunity costs and sometimes has unwanted (e.g. cultural) effects, it will, in certain circumstances, be irrational to introduce them.
>
> That being conceded, one might still insist, first, that innovation will sometimes be rational [for ruling classes], and will therefore sometimes be [allowed to be] introduced, and secondly, that because of rationality and inertia, achieved innovations are very unlikely to disappear, except when they are replaced by still superior techniques. Although people [note the shift back to the general category: RB] are not so bent on productive improvement that they will seize every opportunity of effecting it, they will certainly not lightly abandon such improvements as they have in fact effected. The upshot will therefore be a long-run tendency in every society to productive improvement, even if the tendency does not express itself in each period of every society's history. (*HLF* 26)

The last sentence reaffirms the Development Thesis as holding true for every human society. On the page directly following the above passage, however, Cohen considers a weaker version of the Development Thesis which concedes that "a whole society might, even under scarcity, lack an internally generated (that is, not induced by contact with other societies) tendency to productive improvement, because of standing (e.g. cultural) circumstances" (*HLF* 27). Still, global development continues to be posited, because of external inducement. "As long as circumstances are not always unpropitious in all societies, progress will occur somewhere, and its fruits will be preserved" (27). I shall for the time being continue to construe the Development Thesis in its "strong" form, since (as I shall argue in the chapter to follow) to concede the possibility that a society may lack an internal tendency to productive improvement because of "cultural circumstances" runs the severe risk of collapsing HM, since (according to the content assigned "cultural") it starts a slide toward contravening the requirement that the tendency to productive growth not *ultimately depend on* (and so not ultimately be explained by) what is social.

At the same time, it is supposed to be the case that this stipulated requirement of the theory does not imply that the tendency cannot *proximately* depend for successful fulfillment on what is social. Cohen (in more than one place) emphatically states that HM denies

> that relations of production constitute any part of the ultimate reason why development tends to occur. For it locates that ultimate reason in the facts that people are rational, innovative, and afflicted by scarcity. The conclusion from those facts, that productive forces will tend to develop, would not be true unless social relations were characteristically propitious. But the fact that they are propitious is not why the tendency to development obtains, nor even why, in the final analysis, it is fulfilled, since, in the final analysis, it is because of that autonomous tendency that the relations are as they are. (*HLF* 92).

Cohen, as I have said, repeatedly asserts this position. But the position rests on mistake. The mistake proceeds from two things: an ambiguity attaching to the expression "why the tendency to development obtains", and a confusion (similar to one encountered earlier) between necessary conditions and effective causes.

The alleged tendency to development, remember, is not "a *mere* tendency" (*HLF* 86). (As when, say, a person has a tendency to grow fat, but prevents this occurring by discipline and exercise.) The tendency is alleged to be "*by and large, fulfilled*" throughout the course of history (*HLF* 87). That it *is* fulfilled throughout history is supposed to be what explains the social forms that past societies have taken and the social form present and future societies shall take. According to the theory, societies take (and must take) those forms because those forms are *functional* for the tendency. It follows that if the tendency were to be unfulfilled, there would be nothing for the posited succession of social forms to be functional *for*. At the same time, if the tendency is to be fulfilled at any particular historical time, a certain social form S is needed to enable it to be fulfilled. Being so needed, S occurs.

That, according to the theory, is the explanation of S. But suppose I ask: if it is the case that only if the propitious social form S is present will the the tendency be fulfilled, doesn't this mean that S *causes* the tendency *to be* fulfilled? Cohen's answer to this question (in the writings under examination) is 'no'. One reason behind this 'no' is the alleged fact that S may be functionally explained by the tendency. If S's being propitious for the tendency's fulfillment is what explains S obtaining, then S is not the cause of the tendency; the tendency is the "ultimate" cause of S. However, as we have seen, such an account of S's *coming to be because it is functional for the forces* is only intelligibly explicated by an intentional account of its (and previous and succeeding social forms') emergence, which even HM must grant is not historically plausible. We are left (only) with the admission that certain social facts are needed for the tendency to be fulfilled, and this (to repeat) is admission that these social facts are part of what causes the tendency to be fulfilled.

However, behind Cohen's 'no' is not only the functional explanation appeal but something else, which surfaces in the concluding sentence of the passage under discussion where Cohen reaffirms the HM position that the fact that social relations obtain that are propitious for fulfillment of the tendency "is not why the tendency to development obtains, or even why, in the final analysis, it is fulfilled" (92).

There is something very odd going on here. The first thing to notice is the distinction drawn in Cohen's sentence between the tendency *obtaining* and the tendency being *fulfilled*. I thought the tendency obtaining *was* the tendency being ("by and large") fulfilled? But, furthermore, if, *except* the social relations are propitious, the tendency is not fulfilled, then aren't the social relations, in fact, part of the explanation "why, in the *final* analysis, it *is* fulfilled"? What else might a "final analysis" be other than one that collects whatever *finally* causes something to occur (rather than continue as a "mere tendency")?

It is true that a sense can be given of the expression "why, in the final analysis, the tendency obtains" according to which social relations are not collected by that analysis. This is the sense in which talk of a tendency does not entail talk of its fulfillment (as in the tending to grow fat example above). But in HM, talk of the tendency does entail talk of its fulfillment. Indeed, Cohen shifts, in at least one place, directly from talk of the tendency to talk of what it is a tendency to, with the word 'tendency' dropping out altogether. I have in mind this important passage at *HLF* 158 (a variant of the sentences from *HLF* with which we began). Emphases are mine.

> Recall that historical materialism is the theory which says that there exists, throughout history, *a tendency* towards growth of human productive power, and that forms of society rise and fall when and because they enable and promote, or frustrate and impede, that growth. Now we obtain capsule formulations of inclusive and restrictive historical materialism if we qualify a related statement in respectively different ways: History *is*, centrally/*inter alia* the *systematic growth* of human productive power, and forms of society rise and fall when and because they enable and promote, or frustrate and impede, that growth.

Note the shift from there exists in history a *tendency* towards growth of human productive power to history *is* the systematic growth of such power. To repeat, in HM, talk of the tendency is talk of its fulfillment. But in HM, therefore, if social relations are a crucial part of the reason why the tendency in fact obtains, are they not (tautologically) a crucial part of the explanation why, in the final analysis, the tendency is fulfilled?

Cohen's rejoinder is that the relations do not "constitute any part of the ultimate reason why development tends to occur" (*HLF* 92, quoted above). But this is just another version of the "final analysis" move, and as little persuasive. The reason it does not persuade is that it confuses what generates human beings *seeking* improvement in productive capacity with what causes that improvement to be *achieved*. I can perhaps most easily bring out this confusion by looking for a moment at an analogy Cohen employs to "illuminate" the reasoning of the page 92 passage under discussion.

> One might argue that there will be a tendency for people's illnesses to be cured by other people, who get better over time at curing illnesses, simply because people dislike being ill, something which is not, in the present sense, a social fact. Yet suppose, quite plausibly, that, without appropriate medical organization, which is a social structure, little curing, or progress in curing, would occur. The basic explanation of the tendency of illness to be cured, and of its fulfillment, might nevertheless remain, as was claimed, people's hatred of illness, which could also be adduced to explain, through the tendency to improvement in cures which it generates, the existence of propitious medical organization. (92)

This passage (granting its own hypotheses) confuses what generates people's seeking cures (*viz*. their vulnerability to and dislike of illness) with what generates the tendency to improvement in cures (*viz*. appropriate medical organization). The "basic explanation of the tendency of illness *to be cured*" is not (*pace* Cohen) "people's hatred of illness". That explains, rather, the tendency of people to seek cures for illness. The basic explanation of the tendency of illness to be cured is "the existence of propitious medical organization", i.e. "social structure". To put it differently, we may grant that it is a necessary condition of there being a (fulfilled) tendency to improvement through history that people dislike being ill. But that does not make it the case that their dislike of illness is, "in the final analysis", the "ultimate reason" of there being that tendency to improvement in cures. People can dislike illness all they like (and did, for hundreds of centuries) without there being improvement in cures. Until propitious medical (and other kinds of) organization arose, improvement in curing was not forthcoming. But this is because it was that organization (fostering, handing on, and deploying knowledge and practices of certain kinds) that caused the improvement to be achieved.

Doubtless, except there were the asocial fact of people's dislike of illness there would not have been a "search and selection" for such means and organization as were propitious for improvement. This does not, nevertheless, make this asocial fact the cause of the improvement (the fact being entirely compatible with lack of improvement), nor does it make inevitable such improvement being achieved. What explains the fact that something is desired and sought does not, eo *ipso*, explain the fact that what is sought is got.

In the same way with HM's posited tendency to improvement: we may grant that it is a necessary condition of the tendency being realized that human beings are rational, innovative, and endure scarcity. But these "asocial" facts are not sufficient to explain the fact that this tendency is, in fact, realized. To think that they are is to confuse people's needing and wanting such improvement with what actually causes the improvement by which these needs and wants are answered. That is to say, it is to confuse a "mere tendency" (of people to value and aspire to development) with an actual "fulfilled tendency" (that development of productive capacity occurs in fact).

The implication of all of this for HM's claim that the explanation of social change lies in asocial facts will be taken up more fully in the next chapter. In the final section of this chapter I wish to draw together the threads of the discussion up to this point by returning to the Protestant Reformation example.

7

Historical materialism "sees history as a protracted process of liberation—from the scarcity imposed on humanity by nature, and from the oppression imposed by some people on others" (*HLF* vii). The process is held to be explained by the fact that "there exists, throughout history, a tendency towards growth of human productive power, and that forms of society rise and fall when and because they enable and promote, or frustrate and impede, that growth" (*HLF* 158).

It will be clear that the Development Thesis is the progressive core of HM, positing a continued growth of productive power precipitating successively more liberating social forms. We have also seen that HM is committed to positing continued emergence (however periodic) of those economic and non-economic structures or phenomena that are necessary for continued development of the forces of production. HM offers functional explanations of such emergence. At the same time, HM shrinks from alleging that the Development Thesis implies that human beings consciously strive, and contrive, to institute throughout history just such material or non-material structures as are optimal for the growth of productive power throughout that history.

My argument in this chapter is that HM collapses for want of any tenable explanation of the required emergence of the requisite economic or other phenomena. In his discussion of the Protestant Reformation, G.A. Cohen supposes (for purposes of methodological illustration) that the historical sequence may have been: first Protestantism arose, and then there was selective adaptation of Protestantism according to what parts of it were functional for the autonomous tendency of the forces to develop. But this supposition only postpones confrontation of the problem at issue, since the theory requires that what favours productive advance *will appear* because it has that functional effect. Even if one argues that the Reformation discloses a case of religion first arising in religious opposition to a dominant religion and then being adapted to the requirements of the economy through selection *only* of these parts of it that promoted growth of productive power, HM asserts that these growth-promoting parts appeared (along with the jettisoned parts) because they are so functional, and how to explain these adaptive parts appearing is the issue.

In short (and curious as this may seem), HM *cannot allow emergence of these adaptive parts to be an accident*. If anyone is incredulous at this result, consider these sentences by Cohen, which are revealing in several ways. Emphases are Cohen's except where otherwise noted.

> [W]e can . . . hypothesize that, if Protestant teaching indeed had substantial economic effects, then the features of Protestantism in virtue of which it has those effects *appeared* [my emphasis: RB] in Protestantism because the religion was adapting itself to the economy. We can plead that, even if the commerce-favouring religious changes were *essential* to continued capitalist [and so productive] development, restricted historical materialism is as yet undefeated, since it is a credible hypothesis that those changes occurred *because* they favoured the development of commerce.

> ... The relevant spiritual phenomena must ... be seen to occur *because* of their tendency to have the economic effects they do ... [in contrast to] a merely interactionist view of the relationship between the economic and the spiritual, [since] on such a view there is no reason to suppose that the prescribed line of economic advance will be maintained: it would be an accident if it was...
>
> When we explain spiritual phenomena in this [functional explanatory] fashion, we can, if need be, concede that they [these religious phenomena] are necessary and sufficient, in the circumstances, to keep material development in its theoretically mandated course [of systematic growth of human productive power]. The concession does not contradict historical materialism, as long as the state of the economy was itself sufficient for the emergence *and/or* persistence [my emphasis: RB] of the given spiritual phenomena. But—to repeat the point made above—if it were sufficient for their persistence, but did not also functionally explain them, then it would be an accident that their impact on the economy kept it on course, and that is something which could not be an accident for historical materialism. (*HLF* 164-5)

Note first, here, the express extension of the historical materialist functional explanation claim to one of *emergence*. Note too the explicit thesis that whatever is necessary for productive power to grow must, by virtue of that fact (that it is so necessary), come about. It cannot simply be an accident that it does come about.

To repeat, HM asserts that there is, in fact, a *realized* "persistent tendency for productive power to grow" which is a "result of extremely general material features of the human situation" *HLF*, 164). HM does not assert that productive power tends to grow in the sense of 'tends' that is compatible with its not in fact growing (as where a person's metabolism may be such that he or she tends to grow fat but does not do so because the person counteracts the tendency with a regimen of exercise and diet). The word 'tendency' in HM's thesis always refers to a "by and large, *fulfilled*, tendency for the productive forces to develop" (*HLF*, 87).

More schematically, HM proceeds from the first to the third of these three propositions:

F20. Changes in a society's social institutions that have the effect of facilitating development of the society's productive forces occur because they have that effect.

More specifically:

F21. Spiritual developments that have the effect of facilitating development of a society's productive forces occur because of their tendency to have that effect.

More specifically still:

F22. Certain of the religious developments denoted 'Protestantism' that promoted capitalist development occurred because they favoured that development.

Consider the words 'occur' and 'occurred' in these three statements (which reproduce virtually verbatim Cohen's own formulation of the issues: see the passages quoted above from *HLF* 164, and also lines 5–12 and 32–35 of that page). The past tense 'occurred' directly implies 'emerged'. The present tense 'occur', however, is ambiguous between 'emerge' and 'persist'. Cohen, in his discussion of Protestantism, moves back and forth between 'occur' and 'occurred', reflecting a tendency to treat as unimportant the difference between the two, exhibited graphically in his reference to the state of the economy being "sufficient for the emergence and/or persistence of the given spiritual phenomena". It is true that directly following these words he declares that if the state of the economy "were sufficient for their persistence, but did not also functionally explain them, then it would be an accident that their impact on the economy kept it on course, and that is something which could not be an accident for historical materialism".

But it is important to recognize that by "functionally explain" here, Cohen does not refer to these phenomena's emergence. He refers (note his words) to the economy functionally explaining *their persistence*. Cohen is distinguishing here between the two situations:

S1. The state of the economy is such as to allow these spiritual phenomena to persist, but their persisting is not functionally explained by their contributing to growth of productive power. Rather, they may have no effect on the economy whatever. (A parallel is where the temperature of the air mass over the city is such as to keep the ice cream in my cone from melting, but the ice cream's not melting is not functionally explained by its contributing to the temperature of that air mass.)

S2. The state of the economy is such as to cause these (and not other) spiritual phenomena to persist, and their persisting is functionally explained by their contributing to growth of productive power. It is their contributing to productive growth that causes them to persist. Except they had that effect they would not persist.

In the sentence under discussion, Cohen is supposing the second circumstance. Yet the supposition provides no explanation of how these spiritual phenomena arose in the first place. At the same time, that their emergence is necessary is, remember, the hypothesis from which Cohen began: "that Protestant teaching had substantial economic effects . . . *essential* [Cohen's italics] to continued capitalist development"—" *necessary* [my italics] and sufficient . . . to keep material development in its theoretically mandated course".

The absence here, and throughout HM, of an account (which functional explanation cannot provide) of the emergence of phenomena predicated as necessary by the Development Thesis leaves HM without a tenable explanation of its posited developmental trend.

Chapter Two

Productive Activity and Social Forms

The previous chapter focused upon the claim that historical materialism *functionally* explains the course of social change. The focus of this chapter is the allegation by historical materialism that "the fundamental explanation of social change lies in facts which are in an important sense *asocial*, and, in one sense of the word, material"(*HLF* 83, my emphasis).

1

We encounter here an opposition between 'social' and 'material' facts. This opposition is basic to HM's allegation, since the claim is that something which is material but not social explains what is social.

According to G.A. Cohen, "[t]he relevant fundamental facts are asocial in that no information about social structure enters into their formulation, under the following understanding of *social structure*: a statement formulates a fact about social structure if and only if it entails an ascription to (specified and unspecified) persons of rights or effective powers *vis-à-vis* other persons" (83). In other words, facts are asocial if to state the facts no explicit, or implicit, reference need be made to rights or effective powers of persons.

It is first necessary to appreciate that this explication by Cohen of 'asocial' is not adequate for HM's requirements. Because no social structural facts need enter into the formulation of particular facts (thereby rendering them asocial in the stipulated sense), it does not follow that social structural facts do not enter into the explanation of why these asocially formulatable facts obtain and have the features they do. The facts which constitute the existence and use of the word processor on which these sentences are typed may be described without reference to any social structural facts. Yet it may be the case that only if certain social structural facts had obtained would there have come to be the facts which constitute the existence and use of this instrument. The mere fact that there are facts which are asocial in Cohen's sense is not sufficient for HM's allegation. That allegation is not simply that there are facts (such as that you hold a book in your hand) whose formulation involves no reference to rights and powers (in contrast to the fact of your owning the book, or of Napoleon's being Emperor of the French, both of which facts logically entail reference to rights and powers). HM's allegation is that there are certain facts which cause the course of social change to be what it is, *but which are not themselves caused by something that is social* in the stipulated sense. It is (or must be) this feature of these alleged facts that is especially meant to be marked by denoting them 'asocial'.

In short, we need to distinguish between:

1. Facts are asocial if no information about social structure enters unto their *formulation*.

2. Facts are asocial if no information about social structure enters into their formulation, *or* into their *explanation*.

HM requires that the "fundamental facts" that explain the course of social change be asocial in sense (2), not merely in sense (1). I shall, therefore (unless otherwise signaled), construe the expression 'asocial facts' in sense (2) throughout.

The allegedly asocial "fundamental facts" that are said to explain the course of social change are also described by HM as "material" facts. This latter denotation is intended both to contrast them with what is social (in the now stipulated sense), and also to mark them out as being facts of a 'physical' kind, in the sense that they consist of such things as the capacities of physical organisms (especially human beings) and the properties of inanimate physical objects or stuffs employed in productive activities. However, it is important to note that this appellation 'material' does not exclude intelligence and knowledge. That this is so is obvious from Cohen's illustrative specification of material facts in *HLF*, where he declares: "Examples of material facts in the present partly technical sense are the general one that human beings are able to sacrifice present gratification for the sake of greater future gratification, and the particular one that the productive resources available to European humanity in 1250 ensured that most labour would be agricultural labour" (83). It is obvious that a part of the productive resources of Europe in 1250 consisted of human knowledge, while other parts were the product of, and required for their use, intelligent application of human knowledge. It is also obvious that the deliberate deferral of gratification in pursuit of some expected future benefit is an intelligent pursuit. Indeed, the extent to which material facts encompass intelligence and knowledge is apparent from the category 'productive forces', which we have already seen are defined by Cohen as including not only "tools, machinery, raw materials, premises, and . . . the strength of producers, but also their skills, and the technical knowledge (which they need not understand) they apply when labouring" (*HLF* 4). At the same time, it is a basic tenet of HM that the relevant material facts are not caused to exist by social phenomena. The adjective 'material' applied to facts is intended to mark them out both as physically constituted entities, or properties of such entities, and as asocial, in the second of the two senses defined above.

The allegedly asocial material facts to which HM attaches most importance are said by Cohen to be identified by three "premises" that together allegedly form an argument intended to establish the Development Thesis. The first of these three premises (as stated by Cohen) is that the

> historical situation of humanity is one of material scarcity: given the character of external nature and the forces available for dealing with it, human beings can satisfy their wants only if most of them spend the better part of their existence engaged in more or less repugnant labour. The second premise is that people have the intellectual and other capacities needed to discover new resources and to devise productivity-enhancing skills and tools. And the third premise is that they are rational enough to be able to seize the occasions their capacities create to make inroads against the scarcity under which they labour. (*HLF* 85–6)

I shall return to this passage in a moment. But I first wish to stress that it is upon these three premises that the Development Thesis is said to be based, and that the Development Thesis is the core of HM. As Cohen recapitulates the argument: "In brief: given their rationality, and their naturally inclement situation, people will not endlessly forgo the opportunity to expand productive power recurrently presented to them, and productive power will, consequently, tend, if not continuously, then at least sporadically, to expand" (*HLF* 86).

In this argument, "exclusively asocial premises are used to support a grand conclusion of an asocial kind about the whole course of human history, to wit, that there has been, across that course, a tendency for the productive power of humanity to grow" (83). At the same time, that tendency "is supposed not to be due to the character of social structures" (83). If the tendency should obtain only because of social structures (that are not themselves *materially* explained), it would then lack the requisite autonomy. "The tendency's autonomy is just its independence of social structure, its rootedness in fundamental material facts of human nature and the human situation" (84). Hence HM's need functionally to explain social structures, since only if social forms themselves come to be and persist because of their disposition to facilitate the tendency, can it be held that the tendency is the *a*social driving force of history — i.e., that which explains the course of past historical social change and discloses the course of future social change. (*HLF* 86).

The truth or falsehood of historical materialism depends, then, on the truth or falsehood of the "asocial" claim. HM alleges that it is the "asocially" based tendency to development that causes the progression of "social" forms. It is not social forms that cause there to be this tendency. HM's admission that the development tendency relies upon functionally propitious social forms is held not to count as undermining the one-way determination and explanation, since the coming to be of these social forms is itself allegedly explained by these forms being necessary for the achievement of the tendency. Indeed, the successive coming to be of these forms (as functionally needed) just *is* that progressive course of social change across human history that the "asocial facts"generated tendency allegedly drives and explains. Thus we see how the asocial claim, and the functional explanation claim, dovetail.

I shall mount a two-pronged attack on the asocial claim. I shall first seek to show that among the facts asserted by the "three premises" argument are some that do not satisfy even the asocial *formulation* requirement. Simply to refer to these facts entails implicit reference to what are undeniably social facts in HM's sense. Having established this, I shall then seek to show that the argument composed by the "three premises" cannot plausibly be judged to meet the asocial *explanatory* requirement. Among the facts invoked by the three premises argument are some that cannot plausibly be represented as proceeding from states of affairs that exclude social facts in the stipulated sense.

2

THE FORMULATION REQUIREMENT

The first of the three "asocial premises" asserts "the situation of humanity" to be one of "material scarcity", and connects this situation to "the forces [of production] available" to human beings (*HLF* 85). The second premise declares that "people have the intellectual and other capacities needed to discover new resources and to devise productivity-enhancing skills and tools" (85–6). The third premise pronounces that "they are rational enough to be able to seize the occasions their capacities create to make inroads against the scarcity under which they labour" (86). Recall, before we go farther, that the theory under investigation is putatively a theory of *historical* change. It alleges that certain historically existing asocial states of affairs cause other social (and asocial) states of affairs to come about. Consequently, the theory must throughout attend to what, in the present or past, are *actually obtaining* situations—not to what are only *imaginable* states of affairs conceived and described by *abstracting* features of actually obtaining past or present situations. Yet when we attend to Cohen's formulation of the three premises argument, do we find this to be so?

Consider the first premise. The assertion that "the historical situation of humanity is one of material scarcity" must mean that the situation of every human society prior to socialism is one of material scarcity; a scarcity alleged to arise from the nature of the society's physical environs and the limited productive forces available to it. This statement, notice, is of a very high level of abstraction. When we descend from it to any one of the historically existing human societies that historical materialism purports to address, it is not "humanity" or "society" that we find existing in conditions of material scarcity, but (virtually always) only *some* members (usually the majority) of the society, while some other members of the society, *most often because of their social relation to the rest*, escape scarcity—a fact implicitly acknowledged in the first premise's stating that "human beings can satisfy their wants only if *most of them* spend the better part of their existence engaged in more or less repugnant labour". This fact is connected to another: that in any historically existing human society, the type and quantity of productive forces *actually available* to any specific individual human being or group of human beings—in contrast to the abstract group subject "humanity"—is very importantly a function of this individual's, or group's, position within a network of effective powers or recognized entitlements (what Marx often referred to as the class situation of persons). The word 'available' here, if it is to describe what in fact actually obtains, "entails", to recall Cohen's own words, "an ascription " to the persons in question "of rights or effective powers *vis-à-vis* other persons" (*HLF* 83). We can, of course, intellectually distinguish the whole range of productive forces extant in a society, and speak of these as *available* to "humanity" (meaning presumably the population of human beings whose society we are discussing) at that time in that place. But this manner of attending and speaking does not negate the fact that, in the actual process of social living, what actually is available to any individual or group is, to a very great extent, a function of power relations. And it is, surely, in what actually obtains in human societies that we are to locate the causes of social change?

Unless we are, then, to install "humanity" as the subject/agent of history, the material scarcity (or lack of it) to which any empirically existing members of a human society are actually subject is importantly a function of the position of each within property and other power relations. (It is also importantly a function of existing needs and expectations, and of the kind of knowledge possessed by members of the society, but I defer this aspect to later in the chapter.) To speak of—and to have one's words collect—the situation of material scarcity in which actual historical persons and groups are alive entails implicit reference to rights and powers in exactly the same way that speaking of the situation of material abundance in which Napoleon was for some years alive among the French entails implicit reference to rights and powers.

An analogous objection holds for the reference in the third of the "three premises" to "people" being "rational enough to be able to seize the occasions their capacities create to make inroads against . . . scarcity". (I leave consideration of the second premise until after discussion of the third.) The words 'people' and 'their' in this assertion must refer to members of actually existing human societies, and what it is rational, or not, for human beings living in social relations to do (or attempt to do) is—once more—importantly a function of the existing power situation. For "people" to make inroads against the scarcity under which "they" labour presupposes that they (or at least a great many of them) survive the occasion-seizing activity, and this they cannot rationally expect to do unless the power situation is fortuitous. To put it differently, the only occasion that it is rational for these persons to seek to seize here is one that is created by more than their capacities to discover new resources and devise productivity-enhancing skills and tools. We must avoid a confusion between what is technically possible and what is politically possible. The extant technological capacities of certain groups, or even of a majority of the members of a society, may make inroads on scarcity technologically possible, but that fact is not enough to make these persons' seizing that technological occasion politically possible (and so rational to attempt). What is technologically an opportunity is not *eo ipso* politically an opportunity, and among the human capacities that may be necessary to render rational an attempt to seize extant technological possibilities may be the capacity for *organizational relationships and activities* that are constituted of rights and powers between persons. To the extent that this is so (and Marx's reflections about the relation of democracy to social change under capitalism imply, as we shall see later, that he thought it was so), the third premise encompasses capacities whose specification involves implicit reference to rights or effective powers between persons.

There is reason, then, to judge that the first and third of the "three premises" do not meet even what I have termed the formulation requirement. In each, specification of the facts appealed to involves implicit reference to states of affairs that are social in the stipulated sense. In formulating these facts in such a way as to descend from vague unspecific abstraction to historical actualities, information about social structure is implicitly invoked.

The second of the "three premisses", however, does appear to escape formulation difficulties. The intellectual and other capacities needed for technological innovation are specifiable without explicit or implicit reference to social structure in the stipulated sense. Whether these capacities pass the explanatory requirement is another question. To that requirement I now turn.

3

THE EXPLANATORY REQUIREMENT: Preliminaries

The explanatory requirement is that the facts which allegedly cause the course of social change to be what it is must not themselves be caused (and so explained) by facts constituting social structure in the stipulated sense. To repeat, "exclusively asocial premises are used to support a grand conclusion of an asocial kind about the whole course of human history, to wit, that there has been, across that course, a tendency for the productive power of humanity to grow" (*HLF* 83). This tendency, in turn, is alleged to be the cause of the succession of social forms observable in human history.

Crucial to historical materialism is the tendency's alleged "rootedness in *fundamental* material facts of human nature and the human situation" (84, my emphasis). The claim that the facts are "fundamental" material facts I take to mean, first, that they are facts about human nature and the human condition which are not dependent on, and do not derive from, social structure, and, secondly, that they are just those facts about human nature and the human condition that constitute "the fundamental explanation of the course of social change" (83). Part of what is meant by describing these facts as "fundamental" facts about human nature and the human condition is, then (I am assuming), to distinguish them as asocial facts about human nature and the human condition.

As for these facts being "material" facts, Cohen, in *HLF* (83), refers the reader to the fourth chapter of *KMTH* for explication of this expression. There, at page 94, we are told that:

> . . . many facts which are fateful for society are natural or material, not social facts. Examples: that large quantities of iron ore are available, that railways span the land, that electricity is in use, that half the labour force is employed in agriculture.(*KMTH* 94)

Here too the designation "material" looks to be equivalent to "asocial" (whether in the formulation or explanatory sense is, from the passage, unclear). For the moment, let us assume that this construction is correct. We shall shortly come to a passage by Cohen in *KMTH* which conclusively confirms the equivalence. But let us take it as established and concentrate on what kinds of facts are material facts. In *HLF*, Cohen, as we have seen, cites as an example of a material fact a circumstance similar to the last of the four just quoted, together with an allegedly more basic instance:

> Examples of material facts in the present partly technical sense are the general one that human beings are able to sacrifice present gratification for the sake of greater future gratification, and the particular one that the productive resources available to European humanity in 1250 ensured that most labour in Europe would be agricultural labour. (*HLF* 83)

With these illustrations of putatively material facts in mind, let us return to the claim by HM that "the fundamental explanation of the course of social change lies in facts that are in an important sense asocial, and, in one sense of the word, material" (*HLF* 83). This claim makes it appear that an asocial fact is distinct from a material fact. The facts referred to by Cohen are said to be asocial *and* material. Yet a footnote to this very assertion refers the reader (as already mentioned) to the fourth chapter of *KMTH* for "an attempt to specify that sense" of 'material'. Turning to that chapter we find this passage on its seventh page:

> We may envisage a complete material description of a society—a 'socioneutral' description from which we cannot deduce its social form. It will provide extensive information, detailing the material abilities and needs of persons, the resources and facilities available to them, their scientific knowledge. But ownership patterns, distributions of rights and duties, social roles will go unremarked. (*KMTH* 94)

This passage would seem conclusively to establish that 'asocial' and 'material' are virtual synonyms in Cohen's usage—for whom 'asocial', remember, has only the formulation requirement sense. I shall proceed on the assumption that the word 'material' is equivalent to 'asocial' in this sense.

We have seen, however, that HM requires that the facts it identifies as comprising "the fundamental explanation of the course of social change" must be asocial in what I have termed the explanatory requirement sense. That sense (to recall the discussion of Section 1) is that facts are asocial if no information about social structure enters, not only into their formulation, but into their explanation. Or more fully:

3. Facts are asocial only if that which causes, and so explains, them does not include social relations constituted of rights or effective powers possessed by persons *vis-à-vis* other persons.

Now someone may interject that (3) should actually read:

3*. Facts are asocial only if that which causes, and so explains, them does not include social relations constituted of rights or effective powers possessed by persons *vis-à-vis* other persons, or includes only such social relations as are themselves functionally explained by these same asocial facts.

My response to this anticipated interjection is twofold. First, we have already identified (in the previous chapter) the reasons why HM cannot deploy functional explanation to establish its thesis about social change throughout "the whole course of human history". But secondly, HM cannot, if the theory is to avoid circularity, invoke functional explanation to explain all asocial facts. Yet this (3*) allows. It will not do to specify asocial facts in this way — what (3 *) amounts to:

3**. Facts are asocial so long as that which causes and so explains them are social relations constituted of rights or effective powers possessed by persons *vis-à-vis* other persons, which social relations are themselves functionally explained by *these same* asocial facts.

This specification leads to circularity. It is an ontological requirement of the theory that there first be something that is asocial in sense (3), before functional explanations can be invoked in the way HM proposes. In order for social forms to be functionally explained by their necessary contribution to the development of something more basic or fundamental, there must first *be* that which is more basic and capable of further development. Otherwise, we end up in a circle: fundamental asocial facts are explained by social forms, that are functionally explained by these same asocial facts, that are explained by these same social forms, that are functionally explained by these same asocial facts that are . . . and so on. It must be possible for HM to break out of this circle by positing some asocial facts that are not even *functionally* explained by social forms. Among such facts, presumably, are those cited in the "three premises argument", such as that human beings have the intellectual and other capacities needed to discover or develop new productive forces, are sufficiently rational to exploit these possibilities, and so on.

Thus (3) is the required specification of asocial facts, and discloses once more the sense in which the putatively asocial facts invoked by HM are "fundamental". They are fundamental in being (allegedly) the cause of "the course of social change", because (allegedly) the cause of that productive activity by reference to whose autonomous tendency toward growth any and all (economically influential) social forms are functionally explained.

The question is, are the facts invoked by HM asocial in the required sense? Cohen, in exposing HM, proceeds upon the conviction that they are, or may be, holding that there exist no a *priori* grounds for denying "that extra-social features of human nature and the human situation operate powerfully enough to generate an historical tendency capable of overcoming recalcitrant social structures" and producing continued development of the forces of production throughout human history (*HLF* 106). But Cohen's conviction appears to rest, at least in part, upon his explication of "asocial", according to which, as noted in section 1, "formulation" is taken to be sufficient. This explication of asocial by Cohen goes back to the 1978 book *KMTH*, as we have seen in the passage from that book glanced at a moment ago, and which is worth recalling (my emphases):

> We may envisage a complete material *description* of a society—a 'socioneutral' *description* from which we cannot deduce its social form. It will provide extensive information, detailing the material abilities and needs of persons, the resources and facilities available to them, their scientific knowledge. But ownership patterns, distributions of rights and duties, social roles will go *unremarked*. (94)

Because facts about social form go unremarked in the envisaged description, it does not follow that features of the society detailed in that description are not explained by facts about social form. That they not be so explained is what HM requires. But one cannot conclude that this requirement has been established from mere production of a "material description" of the above type.

Something else in the above passage also calls for notice. Cohen declares that it is possible to give a description of facts about a human society "from which we cannot deduce its social form". This declaration is connected to his "formulation" specification of "asocial". If the description entailed ascription of rights or effective powers to persons, we could (theoretically) deduce the social form. However, once we see that the issue is explanation, not description, of the respective facts, it becomes clear that the question is not whether we can deduce but whether we can infer explanatory social facts from the putative description. The issue, in other words, is not whether there are *a priori* but *a posteriori* objections to the "three premises" argument for the Development Thesis.

It is this kind of objection that I seek to produce in what follows.

4

THE EXPLANATORY REQUIREMENT: The Posited Human Capacities

Recall, to begin, the second of the three "asocial premises" intended to establish the Development Thesis. This premise attributes to "people" the "intellectual and other capacities needed to discover new resources and to devise productivity-enhancing skills" (*HLF* 85–6). Now among these capacities is one we have found Cohen expressly citing as an example of the kinds of material facts invoked by the theory: the alleged "general" material fact that human beings "are able to sacrifice present gratification for the sake of greater future gratification" (83). This ability of human beings clearly must be one of the "other capacities" needed to discover or devise new productive forces and providently employ them. Creatures governed continually by immediately felt wants and existing opportunities for their gratification must be incapable of the kind of prospective activity yielding increased productive capacity that the theory envisages. Suppose, then, we start here.

For HM to pass inspection, this alleged general fact about human beings must hold autonomously of social structures. Yet there is much evidence that the capacity to defer gratification is achieved by human beings only within certain social relations that involve at least effective powers, if not acknowledged rights, of parents and other social actors. Both the most persuasive psychological theories we have, and our own firsthand experience and observation, suggest that the development by a human being of the capacity for gratification deferral depends upon the human being, as a child, encountering and being required to comply with "social structure".

Where a very young child fails to encounter an ordered predictable structure of practice and claims enacted by other persons, to which he or she is required to accommodate, the required capacity will not be developed. If other persons do not engage the child as independent bearers of purposes and powers whose actions and interactions constitute an ordered structure of social relations to which the child is expected and required to take up a *participating* relationship, adapting and shaping much of his or her own practice to that structured interaction of the others, the outcome ordinarily will be a failure on the part of the child to achieve the capacity to defer gratification. If the persons with whom a child spends much of its early life give way before all or most of the appetites, desires, and actions of the child, complying with the child's will in all or virtually all matters, the child finds nothing other than its own presently felt desires or feelings imposing any claim upon its attention, intelligence, and choice. Carried to the extreme limit, such a circumstance may cause the child to lack any capacity for genuinely *intersubjective* relations with other persons, leading possibly to pathological results. For our purposes, it is sufficient to stress that gratification deferral proceeds from *internal* structure, and internal structure (all the evidence suggests) can only be effectively accomplished (by human beings) through early engagement with outward structure. Thus, where from the beginning everything falls before the movement of the child's desires and will, no disciplining of the emotions and will—moral or otherwise—can, ordinarily, be accomplished.

There is reason to judge that the same holds for rationality generally. (I say "generally", since deferring present gratification for the sake of greater future gratification is, or can be, in appropriate circumstances, a sub-class of rational behaviour.) To take the "longer term" view of a matter, and to be willing to put effort into something while awaiting the benefit that effort will create, are among the earliest forms of rationality to which one is introduced and encouraged to acquire. This encouragement to a rational conduct of one's life is ordinarily paralleled by a requirement that one achieve *reasonable* conduct toward others (by whatever criteria those who seek to 'raise' one—a telling expression—judge reasonableness). Reasonable behaviour is another class of rational behaviour, and one in which the capacity to defer one's own gratification out of regard for the claims and gratifications of other persons bulks large. The two species of gratification deferral, the self-regarding and the other-regarding, are exercises of the same capacity, but directed toward different objects, and (to repeat) there is much evidence that most human beings only come to be able voluntarily to sacrifice present gratification of themselves for the sake of greater future gratification of themselves through being frequently required, from an early age, to defer or limit their own present gratification *for the sake of others' gratification*, and to defer or limit their own present gratification for the sake of some alternative or future benefit to themselves, respect for which is elicited or exacted from them by those persons who oversee and seek to impose a reasonable structure upon their childish behaviour.

Throughout, the constant is the presence of other persons, whose exercise of rights or effective powers in relation to the child (and to one another) constitutes a structure of relationship and practice whose demands and encouragements (if they are of the right kind) dispose the child to considered conduct whose observance develops in the child, over time, both the capacity to defer gratification and the inclination to make use of this capacity in the rational pursuit of objectives to which he or she is drawn. The idea that human beings possess self-discipline from birth, or acquire it by themselves, and then extend it to relations toward others, is a conception of "human nature" and human psychology that was fully exposed as bankrupt by Rousseau. It would be curious indeed if Marx held such a view, since one among those from whom he learned much was Hegel, who learned much from Rousseau. Hegel did not for nothing declare that "In his property a person exists for the first time as reason",[1] by which he meant (in part) that it is especially in acquiring a sense of himself as a *bearer of rights and claims* against other persons (which persons must be acknowledged as having claims and entitlements against him) that a child begins to emerge as a reasonable, a *reason-heeding*, subject. Nor did Marx criticize for nothing, as early as 1845, doctrines of social change that overlook the fact that since "it is men who change circumstances", it is therefore "essential" somehow first "*to educate the educator*" (the third of the *Theses on Feuerbach*,[2] my emphasis).

In short, what we know concerning human psychology suggests that a human being needs structure to develop the capacity to defer gratification (whether that capacity be exercised in regard to the person's own or others' wants or needs). Because we can "formulate" the facts constituting that capacity without reference to that necessary structure (which structure is "social" in the stipulated sense), it does not follow that the structure is not causally necessary for the capacity to be developed. Thus while the capacity to defer gratification may be causally operative in history, its being so is partly explained by social structure.

It will not do to try to save HM by alleging that the specific social structure operative here is itself explained by the social structure of property relations, which in turn is functionally explained by the developmental tendency. In the first place, the capacity for gratification deferral is supposed to be *part of the explanation of the alleged developmental tendency*, so this move institutes a circle. We now invoke the developmental tendency to explain property relations, which relations are alleged to explain this other type of social structural relations, that partly explain the capacity of persons for gratification deferral, which capacity was introduced as part of the explanation of the developmental tendency. This reasoning is circular. Secondly, Cohen's definition of "social structure" straightforwardly collects family, educational, and wider social relationships (such as those between a child and relatives, neighbours or playmates) that make up the structured social relations in question. Thirdly, the structure in question is either *ontologically prior to*, or *inclusive of*, a society's property relations. As Rousseau saw, there must first be human beings who are capable of, and who live in social relations with other human beings capable of, rational, gratification-deferring projects, before it makes sense to attribute to these beings a concern to establish a *future*-bearing claim on the use or consumption of some particular resource or object. What HM terms "the social relations of production" of a human society are property relations, and these involve the capacity under discussion, which, in turn, involves social structure of the kind outlined above. Either it is the case that what I am calling family relations alone raise the capacity in question, which is then exercised in property (and other) relationships, or (more plausibly) among the social relations productive of the capacity for gratification-deferral are property relations (which exist within the family and to which a child is early introduced and required to respect). But whichever account one judges is nearest the reality, both contradict HM, since both entail that the explanation of human beings' ability to sacrifice present gratification for the sake of greater future gratification encompasses social structure.

It was, I believe, partly appreciation of this fact that led Marx and many others to conceive of the earliest and most primitive forms of human society as a kind of crude "communism". In this proto-historical claim is expressed the social psychological insight that *private* property claims respecting means of production entail both advanced methods of need satisfaction and highly developed capacities for gratification deferral. The reason is that respecting other persons' property (even under the sole impetus of coercive prohibition) just is an instance of persistent gratification deferral. To suppose that property relations (or their idea) came first, and then "functionally" called into being (either directly, or through mediating forms of social relation) the needed "material" psychological capacities, is like imagining that the omelet (or its idea) caused to exist the eggs.

Indeed (to return briefly to a question already touched upon in the previous chapter) is it not probable that a part of the effect of Protestantism on economic activity in Europe is to be explained by the very considerable capacity for, and disposition toward, gratification deferral that the exceedingly structured and demanding regimen of Protestant family life instilled in the progeny of these unions? If correct, this would make the causal contribution of Protestantism to the rise of industrial economies founded upon capitalist accumulation and ownership relations consist, in part, of the following sequence. Social structure at the level of the family life (including early education and religious instruction) is a basic cause of the capacity and disposition for gratification deferral. The Protestant Reformation contributed to shaping that structure within societies in Europe in such a way as to increase both the capacity and disposition for gratification deferral within European populations. By so doing, Protestantism contributed to the emergence in Europe of the type of society denoted 'industrial capitalism'. (Mere 'capitalist relations' being nearly as old as the hills, and certainly prominent, though not dominant, in Europe by the fourteenth century.) If correct, this surmise also contradicts HM, since a fact about human beings alleged to be among those giving rise to the development tendency is here explained as taking a specific historical form and having a distinctive economic effect because of features of social life and social structure that are not themselves explainable by the tendency.

But even if this hypothesis about the Protestant Reformation is incorrect, it remains true that the capacity for gratification deferral appears to be a fact whose explanation lies at least partly in social structure.

I have suggested that other aspects of rationality are also subject to social structure. We need to take up this broader question in some detail.

5

THE EXPLANATORY REQUIREMENT: Rational Choice and Productive Activity (1)

In cosidering more generally the relationality to social structure it will be helpful to keep in mind four things already touched upon. The first is that many things may together comprise the explanation of some process or event (as we saw when discussing the evolution of flight in birds in Chapter One). Each causal factor may be necessary but not sufficient for the process or event to take place. The explanation, therefore, involves all of them.

The second thing worth remembering is that it is important to distinguish between continuity and change. What explains why something persists through time may not be identical with what explains why it first arose; or why, after a long period of stable existence, it is supplanted by something else.

The third thing worth remembering is Cohen's remark about "a material description" of a society "from which we cannot deduce its social form" (*KMTH* 94). I have already argued that the question is one of inference not deduction. The object of our attention is, after all, an empirical, historical process of social change. Now Cohen himself asserts on the page following the words just quoted from *KMTH*: "Though we cannot *deduce* social relationships from a material description, we can *infer* them more or less confidently, by dint of general or theoretical knowledge" (95, his emphasis). He then gives an example: "To say that a man regularly makes shoes, which cover the feet of others, is to describe him only materially, but it will be extremely likely that he is a shoemaker, occupying a social role with established relations to suppliers and customers, and not, for example, a shoemaking leather thief the fruits of whose toil are regularly stolen" (95–6). Note first that the inference here is to the more probable of two *social* facts. Both sale and theft involve ascription of rights or effective powers to persons. But note too that the inference is to a social description ("shoemaker") from the putatively material description; as we would expect, given Cohen's explication of "asocial facts". Asocial facts are, for him, facts that admit of a kind of description; hence the issue of inference is for him that of inferring a social description from a material description. Our project, however, is to investigate whether the "fundamental facts" invoked by HM admit of social *explanation* — are, that is, facts from whose asocial formulation we can infer "by dint of general or theoretical" or (I want to add) historical knowledge, the action of *social structural* facts in *producing* them.

That is our immediate project. Notice, however, that fully to assess HM's "asocial" claims involves attention to causality in two directions. We must decide not only whether the fundamental facts invoked by HM are, or are not, themselves partly caused by social facts, but also whether these fundamental facts, even if found to be asocial in the stipulated sense, are plausibly represented as the cause of specific types of social form and successive changes in social form. The latter causality issue may be illustrated by a text that has always been a favourite staple of historical materialism: Marx's remark in *The Poverty of Philosophy* that "The hand mill gives you society with the feudal lord, the steam mill, society with the industrial capitalist".[3] This remark is frequently cited as exhibiting Marx expressly asserting that a particular type of productive force (a material fact) causes a specific kind of social form (a social fact), and that change in the first causes a corresponding change in the second.

A beginning has been made in addressing the first causality issue in our discussion of gratification deferral, and this beginning will be continued in what follows. But we must bear in mind the second aspect of the matter, which we shall find surfacing more explicitly as the discussion proceeds.

Bearing upon both causality issues is the fourth thing worth remembering: our brief discussion of Cohen's "final analysis" and "ultimate reason" claims in Chapter One. That discussion arose from consideration of Cohen's supposing a weaker version of the Development Thesis, one which posits that "a whole society might, even under scarcity, lack an internally generated (that is, not induced by contact with other societies) tendency to productive improvement, because of standing (e.g. cultural) circumstances" (*HLF* 27). I remarked then that to suppose that a society may lack an internal tendency to productive improvement because of "cultural circumstances" would seem to depart from HM. It would seem to do so, since if "cultural" circumstances encompass social facts (as our conception of culture ordinarily implies), we have an admission that in some societies the occurrence or non-occurrence of the tendency to productive growth depends upon (and is explained by) what is social. The supposition is that it is because the social facts are as they are that the society lacks an internally generated tendency to productive improvement. But if the tendency to productive growth can be subject to social facts in *these* societies, that seems to mean that where, in *other* societies, the tendency is *not* defeated by "cultural" circumstances, its obtaining is a *contingent* state of affairs whose explanation is in part the (propitious) social facts comprising the cultural circumstances of these other societies. Yet, as we have seen, the tendency to productive growth cannot be allowed to be contingent upon social facts without contravening HM.

At this point, as remarked in Chapter One, expositors of HM are likely to stress that the theory does not rule out (indeed invokes) the tendency *proxi-*

mately depending for successful fulfillment on what is social. All that is necessary is that social facts do not (as Cohen expresses it) "constitute any part of the *ultimate* reason why development tends to occur" locally (or globally). The ultimate reason must be the fundamental material facts "that people are rational, innovative, and afflicted by scarcity" (*HLF* 92).

These, of course, are precisely the facts whose putative asocial pedigree we are about to scrutinize. If, then, we can show that the existence of these facts invoked by HM can only be explained, where they do exist, by reference to the social form within which "people" are alive, we shall have refuted HM.

This refutation is different from that offered in the previous chapter. One might mark the difference by introducing a distinction between what causes the tendency, and what serves the tendency. According to HM, what causes the tendency is not social. What allegedly causes the tendency are the asocial facts that "people are rational, innovative", and so on. On the other hand, what (in my terminology) is alleged by HM to serve the tendency is admitted to be social, but is held to be functionally explained by the tendency. What allegedly serves the tendency are propitious property and other relations. In the previous chapter I argued that HM cannot plausibly represent the social structures that it admits are necessary for the tendency as being functionally explained by the tendency. In this chapter I shall argue that HM cannot plausibly represent the facts about human beings it asserts are the cause of the tendency as being asocial in the explanatory requirement sense.

Both of these arguments assault the theory's alleged "ultimate reason why development tends to occur". One undermines the theory's claim that the ultimate reason is something asocial. The other undermines the theory's attempt to escape admission that facilitating social structures are among the causes of development by alleging that such structures are themselves functionally explained by the theory.

A third, auxiliary argument will be directed, in the concluding section of the chapter, against the theory's recourse to an "ultimate reason" in explaining the alleged tendency to development. But I now return to the "three premisses" argument.

The second and third premisses of the argument for the development tendency cite the alleged facts (1) that "people have the intellectual and other capacities needed to discover new resources and devise productivity-enhancing skills and tools", and (2) that "they are rational enough to be able to seize the occasions their capacities create to make inroads against the scarcity under which they labour" (*HLF* 85–6).

We have already noted in the first premise its attributing a "historical situation" of scarcity to "humanity" (85). We must now take notice of the continuation of this general language in the reference in the second and third premisses to "people" having the requisite capacities, with no qualification as to which people, living when, in what societies, and so on. While the argument asserts scarcity as the (to date) *historical* situation of "human beings", it attributes certain capacities to "people" *generally*—without reference to their historical situation.

This the argument must do, since the argument is, at bottom, that (as Cohen at one point expresses the position) "*extra-social* features of human nature and the human situation operate powerfully enough to generate an historical tendency capable of overcoming recalcitrant *social* structures"—thereby producing continued development of the forces of production throughout "the whole course of human history" (*HLF* 106, 83, my emphases). In other words, the argument pits *asocial*, and, to that extent, *ahistorical* human nature, against social, and, to that extent, *historical* structures of human relations. This, I shall try to show, is a fatal feature of the argument.

Suppose we begin with what I shall term the "intellectual premise" of the argument: that "people" have the intellectual and other capacities needed to discover new resources and devise productivity-enhancing skills and tools. We need to distinguish several different assertions in this matter.

1. The members of some historically existing society S have (by virtue of being human beings) *the potential* to develop the intellectual and other capacities needed to discover new resources and to devise new productivity-enhancing skills and tools.

2. The members of society S *have developed* the intellectual and other capacities needed to discover new resources and to devise productivity-enhancing skills and tools.

3. The members of society S, while now possessing the intellectual and other capacities needed to discover new resources and to devise productivity-enhancing skills and tools, do not so deploy these capacities *because they are preoccupied with, and direct these capacities toward realizing*, non-economic goals accomplishable within the long-established mode of economic production of the society.

4. The members of society S, while possessing the intellectual and other capacities needed to discover new resources and to devise productivity-enhancing skills and tools, do not so deploy these capacities *even when confronted with their potential use to this purpose by foreign nations*, because they (or at least those of their number who have the power to determine social practice in the society) *have no interest* in so exploiting these capacities, because they are preoccupied with, and direct these capacities toward realizing, noneconomic goals accomplishable by means of the long-established mode of economic production of the society.

If assertions (3) and (4) can be shown to be frequently, or even sometimes, true, historical materialism is refuted. Social structures will have been shown to be sufficiently "recalcitrant" to render false the alleged historical tendency toward development grounded on asocial facts. Social facts will be seen to figure causally in the successful achievement of productive development, where it occurs.

Historical materialism will also be refuted if the following assertion is true:

5. Technologies and commitments contributing, over time, to increased productive power in some human societies are frequently caused to emerge, and to be exploited, by forms of social life that are not economic or material as HM defines 'economic' and 'material'.

Assertion (5) is the complement of assertion (4). Assertion (4) claims that social facts are an important cause of some human societies not exploiting developed capacities in ways that foster productive growth. Assertion (5) claims that social facts are an important cause both of human societies developing these capacities in the first place, and of their going on to exploit them in ways that foster productive growth.

I shall seek to show that we have good reason to judge that assertions (3), (4) and (5) are true. I shall argue for this judgment by looking briefly at the history of the mechanical clock and its contribution to the emergence of industrial capitalism in Europe. In presenting my argument I shall draw heavily upon the important book by the historian David S. Landes entitled *Revolution in Time: Clocks and the Making of the Modern World*.[4] This is one of two books by David Landes from which I shall quote extensively in this and the next two sections of this chapter. My reason for quoting from them is to place before the reader an impressive body of historical data relevant to reaching a judgment about the theoretical issues under investigation.

I begin with the question (as Landes formulates it) "how and why so seminal an invention" as the mechanical clock "occurred in Europe and remained a European monopoly for some five hundred years" (11). That the invention of the mechanical clock was seminal, with "revolutionary implications for cultural values, technological change, social and political organization, and personality", Landes establishes in this way:

> [Many societies] had long known and used other kinds of timekeepers—sundials, water clocks, fire clocks, sand clocks—some of which were at least as accurate as the early mechanical clocks. Wherein lay the novelty, and why was this device so much more influential than its predecessors? The answer, briefly put, lay in its enormous technological potential. The mechanical clock was self-contained, and once horologists [clock-makers] learned to drive it by means of a coiled spring rather than a falling weight, it could be miniaturized so as to be

portable, whether in the household or on the person. It was this possibility of widespread private use that laid the basis for *time discipline*, as against *time obedience*. One can, as we shall see, use public clocks to summon people for one purpose or another; but that is not punctuality. Punctuality comes from within, not from without. It is the mechanical clock that made possible, for better or worse, a civilization attentive to the passage of time, hence to productivity and performance. (6–7, emphasis in original)

This is partly right. But Landes' distinction between time discipline and time obedience is puzzling. Punctuality does "come from within", in the sense that a 'punctual person' is someone who is committed (for whatever reason) to being 'on time' in his or her practice. But doesn't this simply mean that punctuality is obedience to a *self-imposed* time discipline? Landes himself has earlier asserted that "The sense of punctuality is inculcated very early, indeed from infancy . . . One of the most powerful notions to shape a child's consciousness is that of being late or of missing . . .—missing a program, missing a meal, missing a religious service, missing a ball game, missing a party" (2). In this sense, punctuality does come "from without", both in that the disposition to be punctual is ordinarily socially-inculcated, and in that the need to be punctual proceeds in great part from facts external to the punctual person. (It is the early bird that gets the worm, and so on.)

What is right in Landes' remarks is his emphasis on the miniaturization of timekeepers, enabling private use. In a later passage, he puts the case for the significance of the mechanical clock much more successfully:

The small timekeeper (portable clock or watch) proved to be a revolutionary instrument. By its very nature it stimulated horological technique, for miniaturization is a school for skill . . .

This technical stimulus was reinforced by the proliferation of timepieces and diffusion of ownership. Where once clocks had been the conspicuous consumption and privilege of an exalted few, two centuries of technical advance and production experience [from the 1300s to 1500s] had now made them available to a widening circle of bourgeois . . .

Even more profound were the consequences of miniaturization for society and culture. Where the people had once depended on the cry of the night watch, the bell of the church, or the turret clock in the town square, now they had the time at home or on their person and could order their life and work in a manner once reserved to regulated communities. In this way, privatization (personalization) of time was a major stimulus to the individualism that was an ever more salient aspect of Western civilization. The public clock could be used to open markets and close them, to signal start of work and its end [each calling for its own punctuality, note], to move people around, but it was a limited guide to self-imposed programs. Its dial was not always in view, its bell not always within hearing. Even when heard, hourly bells are at best intermittent reminders. They signal moments. A chamber [or workroom] clock or watch is something very different: an ever visible, ever audible companion and monitor. A turning hand, specifically a minute hand (the hour hand turns so slowly as to seem still), is a measure of time used, time spent, time wasted, time lost. As such it was prod and key to personal achievement and productivity. (89)

The public clock was a *limited* guide to self-imposed programmes. This is the key feature. The mechanical clock (to revise Landes' earlier conclusion) "made" *more* "possible, for better or worse, a civilization attentive to the passage of time, hence to productivity and performance" (6–7), than did the earlier water clocks, sundials, and so on. The reason was its capability of being miniaturized, making possible its wide employment by individuals for personal use, and a concomitant increase in an 'economy' of time.

At this point a proponent of historical materialism may impatiently enquire how I propose to make use against HM of such a line of reasoning as this promises to be, since the emphasis so far has been on a kind of technological development and its far-reaching social effects. To answer this question we must proceed on two fronts. We must first inquire into how this technological development arose in Europe. We must then consider why some societies exploited it and others didn't. As you will recall from our discussion of functional explanation in Chapter One, it is necessary not only that morphological features facilitating flight emerge in birds. These animals have to act to exploit these features. The same holds for "small timekeepers". The explanation why some societies both developed, *and acted to exploit*, this technology in certain ways, while other societies did not do so, is integral to our story.

What explains the development of mechanical clocks in Europe, when they did not develop elsewhere? (The supposition by Joseph Needham and other historians that China independently developed mechanical clocks is refuted by Landes in the second chapter of his book.) The reader will recall Landes' remark above that the small timekeeper made it possible for individuals, either privately or in association with others, "to order their life and work in a manner once reserved to *regulated communities*". The regulated communities referred to are the Christian monasteries of medieval Europe, and Landes makes an impressive case for the conclusion that it was "the temporal discipline of Christianity, especially Western Christianity" (as expressed in the Benedictine, Cluniac and Cistercian monasteries of Europe) that caused the development of mechanical clocks (59ff).

Christianity is not the only religious tradition that has tied prayer to specific times of the day. Judaism and Islam have done so as well. But in the case of the last two, the temporal markers were natural cycles of time (daybreak, mid-day, before sunset, after sunset, and so on). As Landes puts it, "the times of prayer are bands rather than points". Furthermore, in both Judaism and Islam "prayer is a personal act, without clerical or congregational meditation, and worship, with some exceptions, need not be collective and simultaneous" (59). With Christianity, and especially Christian monasticism, the situation is different:

> For hundreds of years [in the Christian congregations of Europe and North Africa] there were no rules, only practices. Rules came with monasticism—with the formation of a regular clergy (that is a clergy subject to a *regula*, or rule) whose vocation it was to pray and pray often, and in so doing to save that multitude of the faithful whose worldly duties or inconstancy prevented them from devoting themselves entirely to the service of God. . . . The innovator here was Pachomius in Upper Egypt in the early fourth century: against the prevailing eremitic individualism, his new order instituted a minute regulation of the collective praying, working, eating, and sleeping day. . . .
>
> It was in the West, in the Rule of Saint Benedict, that the new order of the offices found its first complete and detailed realization: six (later seven) daytime services (lauds, prime, tierce, sext, none, vespers, and compline) and one at night (vigils, later matins). As the very names indicate, most of these were designated and set in terms of clock hours. Hence the very term 'canonical hour', which eventually became synonymous with the office itself: one 'recited the hours'. (61)

With the Cluniac foundations of the tenth century and the Cistercian of the twelfth century this beginning was revitalized and extended. At the heart of these communities' practice was the *dictum* succinctly stated by Saint Benedict (whom Landes quotes): "Idleness is an enemy of the soul" (67), from which proceeded the submission of all monastic activity to an ordered temporal rhythm, encompassing not only prayer but every kind of work or engagement. As Landes emphasizes, "for monks there was no distinction between worldly and religious" activity: "laborare est orare—to work was to pray" (67).

> Monasteries were beehives of varied activity, the largest productive enterprises of medieval Europe. Brothers, lay brothers, and servants were busy everywhere—in the chapel, the library, the writing room (scriptorium), in the fields, the mill, the mines, the workshops, the laundry, the kitchen. They lived and worked to bells. (68)

These bells had to be rung, including the bell summoning the community to the nocturnal office after a period of sleep. The first mechanical clock devices were "what we now know as timers and associate with three-minute eggs or film developing", but "timers that ran for hours" and "were set to run during the night and served only to trip the alarm" waking the bell-ringer (67).

> It is now generally agreed ... that some of them made use of an escapement type mechanism to produce a to-and-fro motion of the hammer(s) beating on the bell, and that this mechanism was often weight-driven. It is this mechanism, probably, that was the forerunner of the clock escapement. (67–8)

There is reason, in short, to believe that the "monastic clergy may have provided the primary market for timekeepers and the principal stimulus to technical advances in this domain" (70). The church did not, of course, remain the only source of demand, and we shall look at these other constituencies in a moment. But before doing so it is necessary to anticipate and meet the objection that we have overlooked the pertinent fact that monasteries were economic enterprises, which fact may be thought to make the religious context subordinate to productive activity in just the way HM asserts. At bottom, it may be asserted, the driving force behind this (as behind any) technological development is productive activity.

My reply to this objection is that it mistakes an effect for a cause. Consider the following remarks by Landes, which may be thought to support the objection:

> All of this [living and working to bells] was part of a larger process of depersonalization, deindividuation. Monastic space was closed space—areas and corridors of collective occupancy and movement—so arranged that everyone could be seen at all times. So with time: there was 'only one time, that of the group, that of the community. Time of rest, of prayer, of work, of meditation, of reading: signaled by the bell, measured and kept by the sacristan, excluding individual and autonomous time.... Time, in other words, was of the essence because it belonged to the community and to God: and the bells saw to it that this precious, inexhaustible resource was not wasted.
>
> The bells, in short, were drivers—goads to effective, productive labour. It is this larger role, going far beyond reveille, that may account for the higher standard of punctuality enforced by the new monastic orders of the eleventh and twelfth centuries. The Cistercians in particular were as much an economic as a spiritual enterprise (they would not have recognized a difference). Their agriculture was the most advanced in Europe; their factories and mines, the most efficient. They made extensive use of hired labor, and their concern for costs made them turn whenever possible to laborsaving devices.... For such an undertaking, timekeeper and bells were an indispensable instrument of organization and control; and it may be that it was the proliferation of this order throughout Europe and the expansion of its productive activities that stimulated the interest in finding a superior timekeeper and precipitated the invention of the mechanical clock. (69)

This passage may seem, on a superficial reading, to provide more support than difficulty for HM. The opposite is the case. Note first the emphasis throughout on "social facts", on relations of association and subordination to a corporate purpose, which corporate purpose itself proceeds from the agreed subjection of all human claims and purposes to the purposes of God. It will not do to reply that these relations are not "social" in HM's sense. Christian monastic relations clearly involved rights and effective powers on the part of some persons *vis-à-vis* other persons—the rights and powers of abbots over the rest, of monks over novices, of the monastic community over its lands and buildings, and so on. Furthermore, Christian religious life *generally* is social in HM's sense, since it is constituted of beliefs about 'God', an alleged person, having rights and powers *vis-à-vis* human beings and all creation, from which issue obligations of human beings to conduct their life in certain ways, and so on. That God has power and right in relation to human beings is the informing sense of Christian religious practice. Indeed, it is precisely the infinite extent of this power and right that explains the intensity and extent of the monastic commitment. Where we distinguish between economic and spiritual activities, "*they would not have recognized a difference*".

This is crucial to understanding the sense in which the bells were "goads to effective, productive labor". It is a truism among economic historians (Marx included) that there was little concern with efficiency of productive activity both among agricultural and other productive labourers in Europe prior to capitalist agriculture and manufacture. Efficient deployment of labour and materials was something that had to be imposed on agricultural and manufacturing labourers, and the resistance of the populace of labourers to this imposition was a chronic irritant to enterprising economic actors. (Landes explicitly comments, regarding textile manufacture—"the first and greatest of medieval industries"—that there was a continuous "effort to impose time discipline on home workers", but that "the home workers were content to earn what they felt they needed, and in time of keen demand, employers found it impossible to get them to do more, for higher pay only reduced the amount of work needed to satisfy these needs" (73).) Among the few exceptions to this situation were certain of the monastic institutions, whose concept of *effective, productive* labour was (as Landes acknowledges in the words quoted a moment ago) religiously invested. To the extent that the monastery bells operated as goads or "drivers", they did so because of the communal belief in a duty to *husband* time and resources in accordance with the subjection of all activity to the will of God. To work *was* to pray, and so to work *industriously* and *without waste* of God's provision was the duty of the "rule". To do so was also to achieve God's will by putting at the disposal of the monastic community the greatest provision realizable, thereby best enabling it to advance its work in the world. To the extent that the bells were goads, then, they were so in being "visible signs" and reminders of submission to the rule, recollecting and guiding the community to the goals of that submission. Of course, the bells were not only goads—though where the flesh is weak, what is meant to be signal can operate even in the most devout (and with the hearer's gratitude) as summons. We see Landes himself in the above passage stating what he repeatedly emphasizes, that the bells were "instruments of organization and control" (including 'self-control'), required by the monastic commitment to a religious and temporal discipline of the whole of each day. One might sum up the situation by stating that the bells could only be goads because they were guides to achievement of the rule. This is throughout a matter of social facts, and not subordination to "material facts" and "the development tendency" as HM countenances these.

6

THE EXPLANATORY REQUIREMENT: Rational Choice and Productive Activity (2)

The fact has already been noted that "the church alone cannot account for the popularity and development of the new device" (Landes, 70). Other sources of demand were "the numerous courts, royal, princely, ducal, and Episcopal", and "the rapidly growing urban centers with their active, ambitious bourgeois participants" (70). For the first group, timekeepers were a "luxury expenditure". For the second, they were that in the beginning, but as accuracy increased and expense declined, they became more and more an economic tool. As Landes remarks, "Merchants already understood that time was money", and "time shift means clock watching" (91). The result was that a technology which emerged largely in response to the needs of a religious practice was, in Europe, quickly appropriated and developed for non-religious purposes.

Elsewhere this technology did not develop at all; and when it was introduced, it was not exploited for productive purposes. The explanation of both of these circumstances lies in social facts. The most relevant instance is China.

[H]orology is only one of several areas in which the technology of medieval China was ahead of that of Europe: it was China, after all, that gave us paper, gunpowder, movable type, porcelain, and other important and ingenious products . . . (23)

Anyone looking . . . at the world's techniques of time measurement in, say, the eleventh century would have given odds that the Chinese would develop a mechanical clock well before the Europeans . . . But the clock did not come. Chinese horological techniques stood still, then retrogressed. That the mechanical clock did appear in the West, and with it a civilization organized around the measurement and knowledge of time, is a critical factor in the differentiation of the West from the Rest and the rise of Europe to technological and economic hegemony. (24–5)

Landes identifies three main reasons why the Chinese did not develop the mechanical clock. The first reason is that in China, timekeeping was tied to astrological practice, and astrological practice was an imperial monopoly. The "very legitimacy of the emperor rested on the harmony of his decisions and actions with the patterns of the cosmos" (32). Because so, "court astronomers were the only persons who were permitted in principle to use timekeeping and astronomical instruments or to engage in astronomical study" (33). As usually happens when a kind of knowledge is made a governmental preserve because it carries grave political consequences, integrity of practice is supplanted by pragmatic manipulation:

> The important thing was the appearance of knowledge, duly certified to the ruler by the court astronomers and proclaimed by him to the people. The criterion, in other words, was political rather than scientific. (32)
> In effect this was a reserved and secret domain. There was no marketplace of ideas, no diffusion or exchange of knowledge, no continuing and growing pool of skills and information—hence a very uneven transmission of knowledge from one generation to another. (33)

The result was a repeated loss of knowledge and invention, with "each great clockmaker" having "to search in old records for the forgotten secrets of earlier reigns" (34). All this was in contrast to the bordering "barbarians", who, we are told by a twelfth century Chinese memorialist quoted by Landes, "had no restrictions on astronomical and calendrical study", and whose "experts in these subjects were generally better" than the Chinese (33).

Several truths relevant to our inquiry are revealed in this situation. The first is that the political relations of a society must be of a certain sort for a flourishing science and technical invention to be possible. The social structure of China obstructed Chinese horology by subordinating astrological science and horological technology to the dictates of political legitimation and the crosscurrents of factional politics. At the same time, these power relations, resting importantly on social attitudes and judgments, shaped the very conception of time from which the Chinese acted. It is widely known that the attitude of the Chinese toward themselves moved them to repudiate opportunities to learn from other cultures. It was observed by the Dutch Admiral Van Braam who led a Dutch embassy to Peking in the late eighteenth century that the Chinese think that they hold the first rank among all created beings of this immense universe... It may perhaps be supposed that the sight of the masterpieces of art [by which Van Braam especially means artifice], which the Chinese receive annually from Europe, will open their eyes and convince them that industry is there carried farther than among themselves, and that our genius surpasses theirs; but their vanity finds a remedy for this. All these wonders are included in the class of superfluities, and by placing them beneath their wants, they place them at the same time beneath their regard. If, for a moment, they fall into an involuntary fit of astonishment, they come out of it firmly resolved to do nothing to imitate that by which it was produced. (Landes, 48-9)

Instant here is a fact much ignored by HM: the relation of *wants* to *social forms*. The development thesis proceeds as though human wants and needs were everywhere constant, and everywhere operated with the same force. But the actual situation is that what is recognized as of value by human beings, and so wanted, is greatly shaped by existing power relations and commitments. Even kinds of knowledge or practice that could be employed to satisfy important and widespread needs are subject to the judgment of value placed upon them by those who occupy existing positions of power. Hence what is in fact of potential value to a society may be apprehended as a "superfluity" simply because judgments of value, and so of need and want, are ordinarily governed by criteria that are shaped and imposed by the extant configuration of social facts. This is especially evident in the above Chinese situation, since there time itself was appropriated by the emperor as just one more of the universe of things in which he had a property. Landes reports the manner in which even the court society of China, who as much as the majority were without means of marking time, made "sure they came to [imperial] audiences on time". "In the same way that Russian peasants of the late nineteenth century learned to 'catch' a train: the courtiers got to the palace hours early (at midnight for a pre-dawn ceremony) and waited for the drums to beat, the bells to ring, and the gates to open" (51). Landes continues:

The historian Ray Huang, writing of court etiquette under the Ming Dynasty in the fifteenth and sixteenth centuries, tells us that the morning audiences especially were vexatious, trying the patience of all officials, who had to stand about in the open in bad weather as in good, but also of the emperor himself. Some remedy was found by reducing the frequency of these ceremonies; by permitting more appropriate dress on inclement days, and by allowing officials to be accompanied by umbrella bearers. But all these were at best palliatives, and the whole system rested on the assumption that an official's time—*all* his time—belonged to the emperor, who could do with it (and waste it) as he pleased. The only way to correct this waste—*which the Chinese could not even perceive as such*—would have been to recognize [at least some of each day's?] time as private property. This was not a simple

> matter in a system where material possessions were also held on loan, as it were, from the emperor. The position of the mandarin was analogous to that of the apprentice: both were servants and their time was their master's. Under the[se] circumstances, it was not easy to inculcate a sense of time as something to be tracked, measured, saved. (51–2, my emphases]

A concern with efficient use of time proceeds from *competing* projects, claims, possibilities. Where power relations are such that all commanded uses of time are, by definition, *serviceable* to the one to whom all others' use of time is subject, such a concern has little foothold. To get a concern with efficiency we need the judgment by individuals that each has a claim or right to use at least some part of time for some purpose that is either the individual's own or some *rival* master's (God's, say). If all time is perceived as belonging to another, and all commanded uses are therefore service, there is little basis for a perceived need to save or husband time, which is the root of the concept of 'acting efficiently'. This is just another way of saying that human perceptions of what is needed and wanted are logically tied to human conceptions of what can be and is *"own"*-ed, and who can and does own it. Power relations vary greatly between societies precisely for this reason. Despite what (as we shall see in the next chapter) 'historical materialists' sometimes assert or imply, *social* power relations are *cognitive* relations, just in the sense that they involve ideas and judgments. Rousseau saw this clearly in the *Discourse on the Origin of Inequality* when he remarked:

> The first person who, having enclosed a plot of land, took it into his head to say *this is mine* and found people simple enough to believe him, was the true founder of civil society. (Rousseau's emphasis.)[5]

Power relations are of different kinds, and these different kinds may be observed historically to proceed in great part from different ideas and beliefs concerning what can be acceptably subject to power, what are the sources of rightful power, what claims have priority over other claims, and so on. Once a particular configuration of power relations obtains, however, it has continuing consequences for judgments of use and value. From convictions about who owns and so controls what there follows, altogether rationally, interest in some things as worth 'owning' or being done, and disinterest in, or active hostility to, other things whose potential benefit is not appreciated because it presupposes power relations (and so projects and agency) different from those in place. This is the reason why social facts are a basic part of the explanation of economic progress where it occurs. Contrary to HM, *property relations*—in the widest sense—are a basic cause of the presence or absence of technological progress because they directly affect what is perceived as having value or as being opportunity. They therefore directly constitute a favouring or obstructing context for those activities and objects that can advance productive progress.

Nor does the historical record reveal the effects of property relations always succumbing, in the end, to the force of a 'developmental tendency'. We have already seen how in China social facts (as defined by HM) are part of the explanation of the lack of progress in Chinese horology. Progress in human knowledge is a *cumulative* process, and the only way to accomplish this accumulation is through social structures that (wittingly or unwittingly) transmit past and present achievements to each succeeding generation of actors, and empower these persons to be active in the requisite ways. These social structures always involve relations of power, right, and ownership, both among the practitioners themselves, and between the practitioners and other groups or individuals in the society possessing and claiming power. Where, then, there is technological progress, the explanation lies in more than the facts that "human beings" are rational, innovative, and endure scarcity. It lies partly in social facts, which affect what human beings regard as rational to pursue, appreciate as a valued innovation, and even identify as "scarcity".

A further instructive example is the Muslim world. In his earlier and deservedly praised book *The Unbound Prometheus. Technological Change and Industrial Development in Western Europe from 1750 to the Present*,[6] David Landes discusses the absence from Islamic states of an industrial revolution, despite the fact that "the achievements of Muslim science were substantial" (29). At one point Landes quotes the following comments by the student of Islamic culture, G. E. von Grunebaum:

> No matter how important the contribution Muslim scholars were able to make to the natural sciences and no matter how great the interest with which, at certain periods, the leading classes and the government itself followed and supported their researches, those sciences (and their technological application) *had no root in the fundamental needs and aspirations of their civilization.* . . . It is not so much the constant struggle which their representatives found themselves involved in against the apprehensive skepticism of the orthodox which in the end smothered the progress of their work; rather, it was the fact, which became more and more obvious, that their researches *had nothing to give to their community which this community could accept as an essential enrichment of their lives.* When in the later middle ages scientific endeavour in certain fields very nearly died down, the loss did indeed impoverish Muslim civilization as we view its total unfolding and measure its contribution against that of its companion civilizations, but it did not affect the liveability of the correct life and thus did not impoverish or frustrate the objectives of the community's existence as traditionally experienced.[7]

The effect of social facts is also transparently visible in European countries. The consequences for "humanity" of the social relations within which they are alive is exhibited by Spain, of whom Landes observes (italics mine, ellipses Landes'):

> Precious metals and jewels are not productive capital; neither are they edible. But in the right hands, they can be used to command and combine the factors of production for useful purposes. *In the right hands* . . . The silver of America did little for Spain, which re-exported most of it to pay for military operations in other parts of Europe and for imports of food and manufactures from 'less fortunate' countries. Indeed one might reasonably argue that the colonial windfall did Spain serious harm by encouraging her to rely on tribute rather than work. (36)

One could go back even further, to the situation in Europe in 1250, which we have seen Cohen point to as allegedly illustrative of the "asocial facts" thesis. The truth of the matter is that the relative lack then of non-agricultural technical knowledge was importantly caused by the way human energies were directed and encouraged by existing structures of power and subordination, by existing procedures of need satisfaction, and by existing conceptions of need and of the human potential for practical knowledge. The powers and claims proceeding from religious belief and association caused a certain relation to practical knowledge and hardship, limiting or blocking certain avenues of human enterprise, while the existing structures of ownership and need satisfaction contributed greatly to the non-application of human intelligence and natural resources to the work of extending technical knowledge and capacity. To link the earlier gratification issue to this one, present gratification in any society is obviously directly related to existing structures of power and reward, but future gratification too is so linked, where existing structures of power and reward effectively define gratifying enterprise and discourage (or actively suppress) inventive activity whose reward structure would involve alteration of or challenge to existing hegemonies.

In short, there is reason to judge false HM's allegation of a historical tendency toward development grounded on asocial facts. Social facts can be seen to figure causally in the successful development of useful technologies, where this occurs. They are an important cause of societies developing improved capacities in the first place, and of these societies going on to exploit these capacities in ways that foster productive growth. Social facts are also an important cause of some human societies not exploiting available capacities in ways that foster productive growth, even when these societies are confronted with such exploitation by other societies.

One could leave the matter here. But there is a further aspect of this whole issue that I wish to address that is connected to our consideration above of a basic fact about the development of small timekeepers: that they made possible a "privatization" or "personalization" of time that was "a major stimulus to the individualism that was an ever more salient aspect of Western civilization" (Landes, 89).

7

THE EXPLANATORY REQUIREMENT: Private Property and Technological Advance

If there is one historical phenomenon with whose explanation historical materialism must be concerned it is the industrial revolution (as it is ordinarily termed) that took place in Europe, and especially in Britain, from the eighteenth century through to the present. The words 'industrial revolution' applied to Britain and Europe refer to "an interrelated succession of technological changes": "the substitution of machines—rapid, regular, precise, tireless —for human skill and effort; the substitution of inanimate for animate sources of power, in particular, the introduction of engines for converting heat into work; the use of new and far more abundant raw materials, in particular, the substitution of mineral for vegetable or animal substances", such as coal for wood (Landes, *The Unbound Prometheus* 1, 41).

If we ask why there was an industrial revolution in Europe but not in Africa or Asia or the Americas, the answer encompasses a great many factors. The same complexity attaches to the question why Britain was the forerunner in these developments.

To take the wider question first (and in what follows I draw closely upon Landes' impressive study), one basic factor is that by the eighteenth century, several European states had economies producing more than minimal subsistence for the bulk of their populations. This condition was the outcome of centuries of slow domestic accumulation, aided by the appropriation of the resources and labour of non-European societies, and by "substantial technological progress, not only in the production of material goods, but in the organization and financing of their exchange and distribution" (14: note the sensible wider sense given by Landes to 'technological'—relating to technique). As Landes remarks (repeating a fact encountered already in our discussion of China), "Europe imported from the East over a period of centuries a whole array of valuable and sometimes fundamental techniques: the stirrup, the wheelbarrow, the crank (to convert reciprocal to rotary motion), gunpowder, the compass, paper and, very likely, printing" (27) Though many of these techniques came from China, they did not have in China economically revolutionary effects because of the interrelationship between administrative and landowning groups, which caused the continued assimilation of merchants into this ruling class. Development of merchant capital led not to a capitalist class but to reinforcement of the landowning ruling class and continued subordination of the society to the values and traditions that class upheld. (20)

Two further factors forming part of the explanation why an industrial revolution took place in Europe are especially emphasized by Landes, and it is these to which I wish especially to call attention. The first is the scale and effectiveness of private enterprise in Europe. The second is the high value placed by European societies on the rational manipulation of material and human resources.

In Asia and other parts of the world, economic activity was frequently much more dependent upon, and subject to, public enterprise and regulation, especially in the case of water resources for agriculture. In contrast, "the scope of private economic activity was far larger in western Europe than in other parts of the world and grew as the economy itself grew and opened new areas of enterprise untrammelled by rule or custom. The trend was self-reinforcing; those economies grew fastest that were freest" (19). This was especially so in Protestant countries, or among Protestant minorities in Catholic countries, for the reason that Protestantism was "an extreme example of the application of rationality to life", "an imposition of the criterion of efficiency on every activity, whether or not directly connected with getting and spending" (24). At the same time, Europe consisted of a number of competing national economies, in contrast to much of the Orient (and to the Ancient world). A still further factor was that many among the earliest of Europe's capitalist entrepreneurs operated and flourished within autonomous city states, which proved to be "schools of political and social association" and "crucibles for the creation and refinement" of economic and political values "subversive of the feudal order" (20–1). Yet another factor was the growing security of property, both from the state and private persons.

One consequence of all these factors working together was the proliferation of intranational and international trade, which worked to break down the subsistence economy of feudal manors and villages, and contributed to "the rise throughout Western Europe of prosperous cities and towns". Another (related) consequence was "the impulse given thereby to innovation: in an age when the nature and direction of technological opportunity were far less obvious than now, the multiplication of points of creativity was a great advantage. The more persons who sought new and better ways of doing things, the greater the likelihood of finding them" (19). This is the importance of the greater freedom of economic activity in Europe as contrasted with other regions. Social theorists in the West have long been in agreement with John Stuart Mill's thesis that one reason why liberty of opinion is important is because it increases the probability that truth will be found out. But the same is true for technological (including organizational) innovation. A further relevant fact is that the more immediate the personal advantage accruing to an individual's inventive and innovative enterprise, the more motivation there is to attempt and persevere in such activity.

The momentum of all of these facts and developments can be discerned as early as the seventeenth century in agriculture. By that time there was a notable

> [dis]solution of personal bonds and the substitution of free peasant enterprise for managed domains. This in turn laid the basis for what was to prove a crucial element in the rise of industrial capitalism: the spread of commercial manufacture from the towns to the countryside. It was this that enabled European industry to draw on an almost unlimited supply of cheap labour and to produce at a price that opened to it the markets of the world. (18)

The rise of rural manufacture "was the most striking and significant expression of freedom of enterprise", but its development was uneven throughout Europe. A fact of far-reaching importance is that "cottage production for market came far earlier in England than elsewhere" (19).

An important factor in these developments was property transactions: i.e., a market in goods and services. As far back as the thirteenth century, artisans frequently became economically bound to a merchant who supplied them with raw materials and sold their finished product. This subordination of the producer to an intermediary was a consequence of the growth of the market—the shift from production for a local clientel to production for sale on distant competitive markets. Fluctuations in that market deepened the artisan's dependence, since he had often to borrow to survive through market recessions and borrow again to begin production when the market revived. "Once caught on a treadmill of debt—his finished work mortgaged in advance to his creditor—the craftsman rarely regained his independence; his work sufficed [if he was fortunate] to support him—no more—and he was in fact if not in principle a proletarian, selling not a commodity, but labour " (42-3). The drawing of the rural population into the production circuit was merely the extension to the countryside of an already existing economic relationship, but now extended to a group who could be prevailed upon to work more cheaply. Furthermore, rural 'putting out' was free of guild restrictions on the nature of the product, techniques of manufacture, and size of enterprise. There was greater freedom to adjust the product to market demand and to innovate technically. Throughout, the process was most frequently a product of mercantile initiative. (43-4)

The industry in Britain in which the rural putting out system of production first became significant was wool manufacture. By the mid-eighteenth century, "the great preponderance of the British wool manufacture was cottage industry", while the consumption of raw wool in British manufactures grew at a rate of eight per cent per decade, exceeding thirteen to fourteen per cent in the 1740s to 1760s. In the judgment of most economic historians, this is the development that "was the principal precipitant of the changes we denote by the Industrial Revolution", and best discloses "the reasons for British precedence in technological and economic development" (45). These reasons were many, but among the major ones are these.

On the supply side: an abundant supply of raw wool, and a rural manufacturing system unhampered by guild restrictions, enabling the suiting of the product to market demand and to changes in demand. On the demand side: a growing population enjoying an average purchasing power per head and a standard of living higher than on the continent; the absence of internal customs barriers and feudal tolls, creating the largest coherent domestic market in Europe; more equal distribution of wealth and a more open society than continental states, including the absence of sumptuary laws;—all fostering (together with substantial investment in transportation) a consumption pattern favourable to manufacturing growth. In no other European economy was the countryside as integrated into the commercial market. British manufacturers, traders and shopkeepers were relatively freer of customary or legal restrictions, and enjoyed much freer competition respecting price, advertising and credit. Added to these factors were a strong maritime trading tradition, no costly standing armies, the vigourous pursuit of international trading privileges, and colonial settlements treated as continuous enterprises, not short term looting opportunities. (44–47)

Combining with these factors was a prevalent priority given cost-effectiveness against tradition, prestige, and appearance, provoked in part by the greater cohesion of the British domestic market, which created greater competitive pressures, but also by a more widespread commercial sophistication equalled on the continent only by the Dutch. This feature can be seen in the British response to what later featured as a significant windfall advantage: the presence of great quantities of coal. The French, in contrast, for a long time "obdurately rejected coal—even where there were strong pecuniary incentives to switch over to the cheaper fuel" (54n). The British also showed a greater willingness to imitate other people's ideas and practices (in contrast to the Chinese, for example, who, we have seen, held other nations' ways or ideas in contempt.)

One could go on at length in this catalogue. But for our purpose, the above outline is enough. All that it is necessary to show is that the type of social relations (in HM's stipulated sense) obtaining in Britain were *one* of the causes of the industrial revolution that took place there. We have already seen that the historical evidence indicates that it was not technological change in HM's narrow sense that created the pivotal growth of woollen manufactures in Britain, but commercial enterprise responding to market opportunities and causing the extension of existing productive techniques and relations to rural labourers. It is widely established by historians that the move from cottage to factory manufacture—in which the rival cotton manufactures industry figured even more significantly—involved for some time no mechanical technological advances but rather changes in the locale and organization of production that exploited economies of scale and increased outputs through managerial-exacted discipline. But I wish especially to stress one factor repeatedly emphasized by Landes (and others): that Britain generally, and rural manufacture particularly, were comparatively "unhampered by guild restrictions and government regulation", conferring a greater "freedom to adjust and innovate".

The *absence* of a type of restriction or regulation of persons' economic activity by government or guild organizations is, *eo ipso*, the possession by these persons of a right or effective power (*vis-à-vis* regulating authorities and private persons) to enter upon contractual relations and enterprises creating further rights and/or effective powers *vis-à-vis* other private persons. The existence of this situation comprises social facts in HM's stipulated sense. That these were the social facts in Britain is part of the explanation of the industrial revolution that occurred there in the eighteenth century. They are not the whole explanation, by any means. But no explanation that does not invoke these facts could be considered adequate. Nor is this the only place where social facts enter into the explanation in question. Landes reports (as do others) that it was partly employer frustration with worker indiscipline—a situation of effective powers by some persons *vis-à-vis* other persons—that was one cause of the search for and openness to organizational and technological change in Britain. British employers were readily responsive to the proposal or example of "workshops where the men [and women and children: RB] would be brought together to labour under watchful overseers, and [of] machines that would solve the shortage of manpower while curbing the insolence and dishonesty of the men" (60).

Given that there is overwhelming evidence of a direct causal relation between social forms and productive activity that is the reverse of what HM alleges, the question arises: what can account for HM's subscription to the "asocial facts" thesis? In the concluding section of this chapter I briefly address this issue.

8

HISTORICAL MATERIALISM AND 'FINAL ANALYSES'

I have already commented briefly in Chapter One upon HM's recourse to "ultimate" reasons in explaining social change. I wish, however, to explore the matter further here, together with its partner, the resort to "the final analysis".

My earlier criticism was that if we grant that certain social facts are needed for the development tendency to be fulfilled, this means that these social facts are a part of what *causes* the tendency *to be* fulfilled. The only way to get around this admission would be to show that these social facts are themselves caused to exist by the tendency. This proponents of HM seek to do by recourse to functional explanation. On their view, HM is able to represent the social facts in question as caused to exist by their being functional for the tendency. I have already argued in Chapter One that the required emergence of these functionally necessary social facts can only intelligibly be explained by invoking an intentional account of their emergence—an account proponents of HM themselves grant is implausible.

We are left with the admission that certain social facts are needed for the tendency to be fulfilled, and this (to repeat) would seem to entail admission that these social facts are part of what causes the tendency to be fulfilled. In response to Cohen's reply that the existence of social facts propitious for fulfillment of the tendency "is not why the tendency to development obtains, or even why, in the final analysis, it is fulfilled" (92), I noted first that within HM the tendency's obtaining is the tendency's being fulfilled. I then went on to argue that if it is the case that, *except* the social relations are propitious, the tendency is not fulfilled, this would argue that if it is the case that, *except* the social relations are propitious, the tendency is not fulfilled, this would appear straightforwardly to make the social relations part of the explanation "why, in the *final* analysis, it *is* fulfilled". What else (I asked) might a "final analysis" be other than one that collects whatever *finally* causes something *to occur*— rather than to continue as a "mere tendency"?

A further, parallel criticism is that behind this talk of ultimate reasons and final analyses lies a confusion between necessary conditions and what I shall term sufficient causes. We have already seen this confusion at work in Cohen's illustrative passage (quoted from page 92 of *HLF*) about the curing of illness. In that passage we saw Cohen failing to distinguish between what generates people's seeking cures (their vulnerability to and dislike of illness) and what generates the tendency to improvement in cures (appropriate medical organization). The "basic explanation of the tendency of illness *to be cured*" is not, we observed, "people's hatred of illness". That is rather the basic explanation of the tendency of people to seek cures for illness. The basic explanation of the tendency of illness to be cured is "the existence of propitious medical organization", i.e., "social structure". This is the *basic* explanation, just in the sense that except there is such organization there will be no tendency for illness to be cured. In short, while we may grant that it is a necessary condition of there being a (fulfilled) tendency to improvement of cures throughout history that people dislike being ill, we must deny that this fact is a sufficient cause of there being such improvement. That people dislike being ill causes them to seek cures. But the creation and sustaining of propitious medical organization is what causes that seeking to succeed persistently over time.

This notion of "a basic explanation", employed by Cohen in relation to illness, is a variant of the appeal to an "ultimate reason" and "final analysis". The notion is to be found repeatedly in 'Marxism', because the idea of something being the "basis" of something else occurs in a number of passages penned by Marx. Here are two of them, both quoted by Cohen in the fourth chapter of *KMTH*. The first (discussing climate and geography) is from *The German Ideology*, the second from the letter to Annekov quoted earlier.

> The writing of history must always set out from these natural bases [of geography and climate] and their modification in the course of history through the action of men. (*KMTH* 96)
>
> Because of this simple fact that every succeeding generation finds itself in possession of the productive forces acquired by the previous generation, which serve it as the raw material for new production, a coherence arises in human history, a history of humanity takes shape which is all the more a history of humanity as the productive forces of man and therefore his social relations have been developed . . . Their material relations are the basis of all their relations. (*KMTH* 97)

We encounter a slide here from what are necessary conditions of there being a human history at all, to what are alleged to be determinants of the content of that history. The slide may escape notice because of the pervasive ambiguity of the expressions 'base', 'basic', 'basis'.

Unless climate and geography are of a certain type, human existence and so human history of any kind is impossible. That climate and geography be of a certain type is, therefore, a necessary condition of history. Someone might seek to express this fact by saying that climate and geography are the basis of human history. We discern and accept what is meant—provided the utterer does not mean they are the sole basis. However, suppose someone else, hearing both statements, interjects: "Oh, then climate and geography are the basic cause of human history?" Well, yes and no. Except the facts constituting climate and geography are of a certain sort, there cannot be human life.

In this sense, climate and geography are a basic cause of (there being any) human history. But if what is being asked is whether climate and geography cause human history to have the content it does, the answer is no. Features of climate and geography may have effects (even important effects) on human societies, and where they do so they will comprise part of the explanation of the facts comprising those societies' histories. But that does not make climate and geography the basic cause of human history in the questioned sense. They may be said to be "bases" of human history, in the above unexceptionable sense of being necessary conditions of a human history: facts upon which human existence depends. But they are not bases in the sense of *basically determining the content* of human history.—Unless this just means (once more) that they are a basic cause of there being creatures (and so a history of creatures) having the organic nature and capacities constituting human beings; which is just a different way of saying the first unexceptionable thing, and too thin for HM's uses. To treat geography and climate as "basic causes" in the strong, content-determining sense, is to reason analogously to the syllogism: "Except human beings are able to eat there is no human history; therefore, eating causes the content and course of human history to be what it is"; a crude materialism that Cohen trenchantly demolishes in the seventh chapter of *HLF*.

What holds of climate and geography holds of productive forces. It is true that continuity of productive forces is one cause of "coherence" in the history of human societies, if by coherence is meant only that there is intelligible interconnection between many features of social life through time. But to be *a* cause (though by no means the sole cause) of such coherence in human history does not constitute being the "basis" of that history, in the sense of *constituting the basic processes comprising that history*. Productive forces are *a* "basis" of all that comprises a society's history, including its social relations, just in that, except a society has some productive forces, it cannot continue to exist. But from this fact there is no concluding that productive forces are "*the* basis of all their relations", in the sense of being the basic determiner of the content of those relations. Productive forces are only a basis in being one among several necessary conditions of social existence. To be such a necessary condition is not to be a basis in the sense HM proposes. It is, rather, to be a "base" in the sense in which propitious geography and climate may be said to be among the bases, or "basic causes", of human existence.

The expressions 'base', 'basis' and 'basic cause', in sum, are mercurial, and it is especially important not to slide from the necessary-condition sense of 'basic cause' to the basic-determiner sense of 'basic cause'. The same holds for the expressions 'ultimate reason' and 'final analysis'. If someone says that the ultimate reason there is a human history is the fact that the planet is the propitious environment it is, there is no *especial* reason for quarrel here (though why stop there, and not include the fact of the sun, or the galaxy, or the big bang, or whatever?) However, if someone means by these words that when we examine the whole stretch of causal processes constituting human history as these extend from the present backwards into the past, and from the macro-level to the microlevel, we discover climate and geography causing the content of human history to be what it is, there are grounds for extensive quarrel. Yet, in my judgment, just such errors involving these expressions 'final analysis', 'ultimate reason', 'basic explanation', are (if you'll pardon the word) an important basis of the historical materialist conviction that "asocial", "material" facts are the *basic, fundamental, ultimate* cause of the course of social change.

Two other things which appear to form part of the basis of this conviction are subscription to a distinction between "form" and "matter" that is vaguely reminiscent of Aristotle and a kind of "idealism" that is reminiscent of Hegel. Directly following his quotation of the sentences from Marx's letter to Annekov discussed above (in which Marx declares material relations to be the basis of all other social relations), Cohen goes on to assert:

> The relation between man and nature is 'mediated' by the social form: it does not occur outside it. The development of nature, described in socio-neutral terms, is therefore an abstraction. But it is a theoretically important abstraction. For central features of social institutions are explained by their contribution to the transformation of nature. Productive power is socially developed, but it is natural in character. Even scientific knowledge, though nurtured socially, is a natural power of the species man. (*KMTH* 97–8)

Note the admission here that scientific knowledge is nurtured socially. This is an admission that social structure is one cause of progress in such knowledge. Juxtaposed to this admission is the seemingly deflating assertion that such knowledge is nevertheless a natural power of the human species. It may be thought that this assertion can mean nothing more than that except human beings had a biological nature enabling them to achieve knowledge of this kind, there wouldn't be scientific knowledge. Nature is the 'basis' of science in just this truistic sense.

Yet that proponents of HM (as instanced by Cohen in *KMTH*) mean something more than this by the assertion is apparent from what Cohen goes on to say directly following the above remarks (italics are Cohen's):

> We are arguing that the familiar distinction between forces and relations of production is, in Marx, one of a set of contrasts between nature and society. Commentators have failed to remark how often he uses 'material' as an antonym of

> 'social' and of 'formal', how 'natural' belongs with 'material' against 'social', and how what is described as material also counts as the 'content' of some form. (Other terms of the material vocabulary are 'human', 'simple', and 'real', while 'historical' and 'economic' consort with 'social'.) The upshot of these oppositions and identifications is that *the matter or content of society is nature, whose form is the social form.* Marx's materialism is perhaps several things, but the explanation of social history as serving material development is certainly one of them. (98)

The first thing to attend to in this passage is the seeming equation of the matter/form claim asserted by the italicized words with the functional explanation claim asserted in the sentence directly following it. The next thing to notice is that the italicized words assert that the content of society is not (as one would expect) something social, but rather nature—which we have just been repeatedly told is the opposite of what is social. What is social in society, we are invited to believe, is only the "form" society takes.

Surely there is something strange in this? How can the content of *society* not be 'the social' in human life? On the other hand, how can the form social relations take not be the content of 'society', the *social* reality to which we are supposed to be attending? Yet the passage opposes the content of society to its form, alleging that the first is non-social 'matter' and the second 'social' form. We appear to have here an echo of Aristotle's distinction between matter and form, about which I shall say only that this distinction has no uses for *empirical, causal* explanation. Aristotle himself distinguished between formal causation (what is it about a thing that makes it the kind of thing it is) and effective causation (what is it that causes this kind of thing to exist). Furthermore, to the extent that the passage's employment of a matter/form distinction derives from Aristotle, it is back to front. In Aristotle it is the form that is the (formal) cause of the matter being the thing it is, whereas in the sentences under discussion it appears to be the matter that causes the form to be what it is.

It appears that way. But there is reason to think (and here I move to the idealist feature mentioned above) that we do not find asserted here a causal relation. The evidence suggesting this is some commentary Cohen proceeds to produce on a remark by Marx in the *Grundrisse* in which Marx speaks of "the process of production in general, occurring in all states of society, that is, without historical character, *human* if you please". (*KMTH* 99. The last three words are in English in Marx's manuscript.)

However, before turning to Cohen's gloss on this remark by Marx, it is worth noting briefly that *there has never been, and never will be*, any such "process of production" as Marx speaks of. The only processes of human production that there have been, are now, and will be in the future, are ones with a "historical character". What then could be the importance of these words by Marx to our understanding of *historical* materialism—this theory of *historical* change? Cohen's answer to this question is as follows. (Italics in original.)

> Viewed physically [i.e., materially], production appears stripped of its social form [i.e., of relations involving rights or effective powers], and that is how it is described in the chapter of Capital whose task is 'to consider the labourprocess independently of the form it assumes under given social conditions'. Production in its asocial aspect is 'material production', this being the content of capitalist or any other form of production. And that content may be described [note the word: RB] in illuminating abstraction from the form with which it is integrated. We then observe what Marx strikingly calls . . . [and here we have the Grundrisse words quoted above]. So if we look through the social form we discern something conceptually [note the word] separate from it: the human—here opposed to social—interaction with nature which is material production. Having 'nothing to do with the social form' [Cohen is here quoting Marx] it is 'the productive activity of human beings in general, by which they promote their interchange in nature, divested not only of every social form and well defined character, but even in its bare natural existence, independent of society, removed from all societies . . . an expression and confirmation of life which the still nonsocial man in general has in common with the one who is in any way social.' Social man has relations with nature and with other men which are not social but, 'if you please, human'. (KMTH 98-9)

It will now be apparent why I suggested that a kind of 'idealist' thought seems to underlie the passages under consideration. The remarks just quoted provoke in me remembrance of Marx's own early, 1843 pronouncement against Hegel, that "*man* is not an abstract being squatting outside the world".[8] In the same way, I want to say that there are no such "human beings in general" as this passage speaks of, "independent of society, removed from all societies"; just as there is no such "productive activity of human beings in general" which is without any historical character and through which human beings have promoted their interchange with nature. Should the reader expect this to be disputed by proponents of HM, Cohen's own next words directly following those just quoted are (surprisingly, and yet also not surprisingly) these. (Italics here are mine.)

> Material production does not occur in history except enveloped in a social form, for 'non-social man', if he ever existed, disappeared when history began. Hence the purely material process is [and here Cohen quotes from the Grundrisse] an 'abstract conception which does not define any of the actual historical stages of production'. (99)

In that case, I want to say, this so-called "material process" is of no interest to *us* whatever. As Wittgenstein remarked, a wheel that doesn't turn is not part of the mechanism. This wheel not only does not turn. It does not even exist, being a mere intellectual "abstraction", "conceptually separate" from the actual historical process of production and social change that HM purports to explain.

At the same time, these remarks by Cohen about the "material process" undeniably have some basis in statements by Marx himself. This brings us to the question addressed in the next chapter: did Marx himself, then, hold the "Marxist" theory of social change that is "historical materialism"?

Chapter Three

The Theory, Not the Theorist: The Case of Marx

Readers of Marx are virtually unanimous in judging that he put forward a theory of historical change. But there has been much disagreement about what that theory is. In seeking to settle the argument, people have frequently appealed to Marx's own statements about what his researches have established. Surely (many have thought it reasonable to assume), we may look to the author of a theory as the final authority concerning what that theory affirms? I shall argue that this supposition is false not only in principle, it is false, in fact, with respect to Marx. I shall seek to show that Marx frequently produced, and accepted from others, importantly erroneous characterizations of his explanation of historical change. His understanding of why and how societies undergo fundamental social change is not, I shall argue, to be found in Marx's descriptions of the theory he produced. It is to be found in the explanations he produces of specific instances of historical change.

I shall begin my argument by examining a lengthy (but, to my knowledge, little discussed) description of Marx's theory which he himself openly endorsed. The description is to be found in Marx's "Afterword" to the 1873 second edition of the first volume of *Capital*. This Afterword is, as I have said, rarely, if ever, discussed (I myself have never seen an examination of the passages I shall consider), except for a few sentences at the the very end of it, which are often quoted. These are the sentences in which Marx describes his "method" as a "dialectical method" deriving from Hegel, whom Marx speaks of as "that mighty thinker" who, despite the "mystification which the dialectic suffers in Hegel's hands", was "the first to present its general forms of motion in a comprehensive and conscious manner" (102–3). With Hegel, Marx declares, the dialectical method is "standing on its head" (meaning, roughly, that everything is represented as proceeding from ideas). "It must", Marx declares, "be inverted, in order to discover the rational kernel within the mystical shell".

For the moment, there is no need for us to go into the issue of what is meant by the "dialectic", or to sort out the mixed metaphors in which Marx speaks of it here. We shall attend briefly to Marx's description of his method as 'dialectical' later in the chapter. At this stage it is enough to be aware that the description implies that there is a 'logic' to historical events, which can be discerned, and whose content and movement it is the objective of the social theorist to identify and articulate. What I wish to focus upon in the Afterword is not Marx's talk of dialectic but his reproduction of a long description of his method and results by Professor I.I. Kaufman, an economist at the University of St. Petersburg, in a review of the Russian translation of *Capital* that had appeared in 1872. After setting out that description, I shall proceed to set beside it a selection of passages from Marx's writings in which he explains a variety of historically significant social phenomena and events. I shall draw these passages from three early writings: *The Communist Manifesto*, written in 1845–6, *The Eighteenth Brumaire of Louis Bonaparte*, dating from 1852, and two essays on India written in 1847. I shall seek to show that as early as the mid-1840s we find Marx giving explanations of important historical developments that are in opposition to the pronouncements found in the lengthy description of his theory that I shall examine. After considering these early writings, I shall then examine what is doubtless the most famous statement by Marx of his theory, the perennially quoted passage from his preface to the 1859 *A Contribution to the Critique of Political Economy*. My reason for looking briefly at the 1859 preface statement is not so much its fame as the fact that it, too, was thought sufficiently well of by its author to be recycled in the first volume of *Capital* (in a footnote to the opening chapter). It is therefore appropriate to recall that statement toward the end of this chapter's discussion, because in the chapter to follow I shall seek to show that it is precisely Volume One of *Capital* that most completely explodes the claim of these famous 1859 sentences to attention. In considering the 1859 preface we shall also take up briefly the issue of "the dialectic" in Marx's theory.

Before turning to Marx, however, it is necessary to establish what I have merely asserted above: that there is no infallible authority assignable a theorist's statement of the content of his or her own theory. My argument here will be brief and elementary, and a reader who already grants the fact may wish to pass over the next section and turn directly to section 2.

1

It has long been recognized that in moral assessments of the character of human beings, or of their interactions with other persons, the individuals whose actions or character are to be assessed are not themselves in any especially privileged position as assessors. On the contrary, everyone readily acknowledges that the persons who are to be assessed are at least as vulnerable to misjudging their own acts or character as is any disinterested but informed observer. It is a fact about human beings that they can be mistaken or deluded about the moral quality of their own acts and character, and even about their own feelings toward other people. A man may think that there is nothing of resentment or untruthfulness in his relations to a parent, though a friend may see much that reveals both. Moreover, the man himself may come (with or without the friend's help) to recognize that this is so. He may come to acknowledge that *his own relation* to his parent he failed to appreciate correctly. To state the matter most simply, we all agree upon the importance of distinguishing between "*X thinks* that he has moral qualities A, B, C, or that he is free of feelings D, E, F" and "*X has* moral qualities A, B, C, and is free of feelings D, E, F". This distinction is, of course, simply an instance of the elementary difference between the two situations:

X thinks that P is the case.

P is the case.

Hamlet's tag to the contrary, there are few things of which it is true that merely thinking them makes them so. Included in that recalcitrant majority are theories.

A theory is an explanation of something. My theory of why bread rises, or seeds germinate, or crime increases, is my explanation of how these phenomena occur. It follows that if a writer gives explanations of phenomena, those explanations constitute his or her theory about those phenomena. At the same time, these explanations may not be identical with what the theorist thinks and says is his or her theory of those phenomena. Consequently we need to distinguish between:

3. This theorist says that her theory about what explains phenomena of type S is T.

4. This theorist's explanations of specific phenomena of type S imply theory T.

There is no necessary coincidence of (3) and (4). One reason why there is not is that the statement of a theory is ordinarily a statement in general terms of processes or relations that must be given specific content in the explanations that the theorist gives of particular instances of the phenomena under investigation. Thus, to take Darwin's theory of the origin of species, one statement of that theory might be: over very long periods of time, morphological features of organisms are selected according to their enhancement or diminishment of the survival and reproductive success of each type of organism in the environment it inhabits, with the consequence that as environments differ and change, organisms differ and change. There is no mention in this (crude) statement of the theory of what particular features of any specific environment have caused this or that specific type of organism to be abundantly present and skeletally different from fossil remains of related organisms previously inhabiting the area. But quite apart from this fact about the generality of theory statements, (3) logically does not entail (4), any more than "This theorist says that her collegial relations are free of envy" entails "This theorist's collegial relations are free of envy".

We may illustrate the above situation with the following simple example. Let us suppose that theories are most often first posited as hypotheses, and then tested against the evidence. Surely, someone might insist, the theorist who makes up a theory knows, if anyone does, the content of the theory he or she has made up? Probably. But suppose we go farther and test this theory (call it T) against the theorist's own practice when he or she is explaining particular instances of the phenomena about which T purportedly is his or her theory. Let us imagine the following sequence:

1. M frames theory T respecting phenomena of type S.

2. M investigates a wide range of phenomena of type S.

3. In the majority of cases investigated, the explanation arrived at by M of some particular phenomenon of type S is not T but V.

4. M repeatedly pronounces that the theory established by his enquiries and forming the basis of his investigative practice is T.

What are we to say is M's theory? Are we to say it is the theory he reports himself as holding and establishing? Or are we rather to say it is the theory implied by the explanations he repeatedly gives of the phenomena he is investigating?

Surely we should wish to say the latter, not the former? In any case, it is this that I want to say (and establish) of Marx. But it is important to see that there is nothing *greatly* strange in any of this. Explaining is something human beings do. A person arriving at an explanation of a particular event is no less fallible a judge and reporter of what that explanation entails at a more general theoretical level than is any other human agent respecting his or her doings.

To mistake the general theoretical implications of particular explanations is a perfectly ordinary occurrence among human investigators. It is an occurrence made even more probable when the person begins his or her career as an investigator with theoretical assumptions and polemical intentions that incline the person to anticipate quite specific results. The probability of such an occurrence is increased further if the investigator's theoretical (and political) convictions fuel an expectation (and desire) that the investigation will establish the necessity, and so inevitability, of processes and developments that are the expected (and desired) finding of the inquiry. Such assumptions, intentions, and expectations make an inquirer more than ordinarily vulnerable to carrying on his or her inquiry with one hand, and writing out advertisements of his or her 'results' with the other.

2

The question that now naturally arises is whether anything like the kinds of theoretical assumptions, polemical intentions, and investigative expectations just spoken of are attributable to Marx. The whole of this chapter bears on this question, but we may consider briefly, here at the start, some statements by Marx taken from what are usually termed the *Economic and Philosophical Manuscripts*, begun in Paris in 1844. The opening paragraph of Marx's preface to this group of writings reads (all emphases are Marx's unless otherwise indicated):

> I have already given notice in the *Deutsch-Franzosische Jahrbucher* of the critique of jurisprudence and political science in the form of a critique of the *Hegelian* Philosophy of Right. In the course of elaboration for publication, the intermingling of criticism directed only against speculation [that is, against Hegel's theory] with criticism of the various subjects themselves [about which Hegel theorized] proved utterly unsuitable, hampering the development of the argument and rendering comprehension difficult. Moreover the wealth and diversity of the subjects to be treated, could have been compressed into *one* work only in a purely aphoristic style; while an aphoristic presentation of this kind, for its part, would have given the *impression* of arbitrary systematizing. I shall therefore issue the critique of law, ethics, politics, etc. in a series of distinct independent pamphlets, and at the end try in a special work to present them again as a connected whole showing the interrelationship of the separate parts, and finally, shall make a critique of the speculative elaboration of that material. For this reason it will be found that the *interconnection* between political economy and the *state, law, ethics, civil life*, etc. [my emphases] is touched on in the present work only to the extent to which political economy itself *ex professo* [by virtue of its especial province] touches on these subjects.[1]

We have here the prospectus of a body of work of very considerable ambition, whose statement exhibits a naive sense of the project's extent and demands (pamphlets, no less!), and in which there is already an emphatic stress on the central role of "political economy" in explaining the phenomena to be investigated. A reader who proceeds further in the manuscripts finds this emphasis continuing, until he or she comes to two paragraphs in the section on "Private Property and Communism" in which Marx—whose appealing humanism and severe condemnation of injustices in the existing social order have already become apparent—remarks (emphases are again Marx's unless indicated):

> That the entire [social] revolutionary movement necessarily finds both its empirical and its theoretical basis in the movement of *private property*—in that of the economy, to be precise—is easy to see.
>
> This *material*, immediately *sensuous* private property is the material sensuous expression of *estranged* human life. Its movement—production and consumption—is the sensuous revelation of the *movement of all production hitherto* [my emphasis]—i.e., the realization or the reality of man. Religion, family, state, law, morality, science, art, etc., [note the scope], are only particular *modes of production* [my emphasis], and fall under its *general law* [my emphasis again].

The next sentence then declares (all emphases Marx's):

> The positive transcendence of *private property* as the appropriation of *human* life is, therefore, the positive transcendence of all estrangement—that is to say, the return of man from religion, family, state, etc., to his *human*, i.e., *social* mode of existence.

Note the assertion (however vaguely formulated) in these passages of a particular thesis, of which the writer is evidently either already passionately convinced (all those underlinings in the manuscript are not there for nothing), or is passionately determined to find true. (Underlining may be a device for silencing unease as to exactly how one's convictions are to be established.) This thesis, furthermore, is expressed in deliberate opposition to a then dominant Hegelian orthodoxy.

These signs do not augur the happiest beginning for so ambitious an undertaking. Ironically, Marx seeks early to dispel any unease the reader may have about the credibility of the pages to follow by announcing, directly after the opening paragraph quoted above:

> It is hardly necessary to assure the reader conversant with political economy that my results have been won by means of a *wholly empirical* analysis based on a *conscientious critical study of political economy*. [My emphasis.]

This, from a young man of twenty-six who three years before was a subscriber to much of Hegelian orthodoxy, and who himself later informs us in the famous 1859 Preface to the *Critique*, had only two years before, in 1842, "experienced for the first time" (while editor of the newspaper *Rheinische Zeitung*) "the embarrassment of having to take part in discussions on so-called material interests", in connection with "proceedings of the Rhenish Landtag on thefts of wood and parcelling of landed property".[3]

With these early pages in mind, let us now turn to three decades later.

3

Consider what Professor I.I. Kaufman, reviewing (anonymously) the first volume of *Capital* in Russian translation, said about the book and its author in the May 1872 issue of the St. Petersburg *European Messenger*:

> The one thing which is important for Marx is to find the law of the phenomena with whose investigation he is concerned; and it is not only the law which governs these phenomena, in so far as they have a definite form and mutual connection within a given historical period, that is important to him. Of still greater importance to him is the law of their variation, of their development, i.e., of their transition from one form into another, from one series of connections into a different one. Once he has discovered this law, he investigates in detail the effects with which it manifests itself in social life... Consequently, Marx only concerns himself with one thing: to show, by an exact scientific investigation, the necessity of successive determinate orders of social relations and to establish, as impeccably as possible, the facts from which he starts out and on which he depends. For this it is quite enough, if he proves, at the same time, both the necessity of the present order of things, and the necessity of another order into which the first must inevitably pass over; and it is a matter of indifference whether men believe or do not believe it, whether they are conscious of it or not. Marx treats the social movement as a process of natural history, governed by laws not only independent of human will, consciousness and intelligence, but rather, on the contrary, determining that will, consciousness and intelligence... If the conscious element plays such a subordinate part in the history of civilization, it is self-evident that a critique whose object is civilization itself can, less than anything else, have for its basis any form or any result of consciousness.[4]

These assertions about Marx's intentions and method in Volume One of *Capital* are notable precisely because Marx himself quotes them (and many more from the same review) in his "Afterword" to the second edition of his book published in Germany in 1873. Moreover, having quoted them, Marx endorses them. Directly following his extended quotation from the review (running to roughly a page and a half of text), Marx comments: "Here the reviewer pictures what he takes to be my own actual method, in a striking and, as far as concerns my own application of it, generous way". Marx does quarrel with some earlier sentences in the review in which the reviewer charges that in his "presentation" of his subject "Marx is the most ideal of ideal[ist] philosophers, always in the German, i.e., the bad sense of the word". However, what I want to stress here is that in respect of the reviewer's substantive account of the book, Marx, so far from quarrelling with it, appears pleased and even flattered by it, deeming it "generous".

The *European Messenger's* review attributes to Marx the following propositions:

M1. The present arrangements of any society exist necessarily. That is, they could not have been otherwise than they are.

M2. It will necessarily come to pass that these present arrangements will be succeeded by a new social order.

M3. What causes an existing social order to pass over into another social order is a process that is governed by laws that are independent of human will, consciousness, and intelligence.

M4. Indeed, human will, consciousness, and intelligence are themselves determined by the same laws that govern the process causing an existing social order to pass over into another social order.

M5. A critique whose object is civilization itself cannot have for its basis [that is, cannot base its explanations upon] any form or any result of consciousness.

Readers may recognize in some of these propositions vaguely familiar variants of the kind of charges it has been common to hear directed at Marx: that he believed in 'historical inevitability'; that he was a 'materialist' who denied not only God but human agency, and who viewed consciousness and ideas as mere 'epiphenomena' determined by 'forces of production' and by other 'material bases' of history; that he therefore regarded not only 'religion' but 'morality' as bourgeois 'illusions' destined to disappear with socialism; and so on. The fact that Marx himself goes out of his way to reproduce, in his own book, comment on it which does seem undeniably to represent M1 through M5 as fundamental tenets of his position may seem to give credence to these charges. Certainly Marx's apparent acceptance of this "striking" picture of his theoretical position might seem to many to be conclusive grounds for taking M1 to M5 as accurate statements of Marx's theory of social change.

I have already given reasons for resisting this conclusion on principle. I want now to undertake the separate task of establishing that the conclusion is not warranted in fact. I shall proceed by examining a number of passages from Marx's writings to see whether they support the judgment that M1 to M5 are accurate statements of his position.

I propose to begin by testing M3 and M4, weighing them first against *The Eighteenth Brumaire of Louis Bonaparte*, written in 1851–2, in which we find Marx seeking as a political and social historian to explain the recent successful *coup d'etat* by Louis Bonaparte in France, and after against a pair of short essays by Marx on British rule in India, published in the summer of 1853.

Before looking at these writings, however, we need to identify more clearly the content of M3. That proposition, remember, asserts the following:

M3. What causes an existing social order to pass over into another social order is a process that is governed by laws that are independent of human will, consciousness, and intelligence.

This statement may be read in at least two ways. It may be read as asserting:

M3A. The process causing one social order to be succeeded by another is governed by laws that are not subject to human will, consciousness, and intelligence.

Or, M3 may be read as asserting the different proposition:

M3B. The process causing one social order to be succeeded by another is governed by laws whose operation does not involve human will, consciousness, and intelligence.

On the first construction, M3A, the assertion that the (alleged) laws are "independent" of human will, consciousness, and intelligence is still compatible with consciousness, intelligence, and will being involved in the process, but in ways subject to these laws. On the second, and more extreme, construction, M3B, the alleged laws govern processes into which human will, consciousness and intelligence do not even enter. Which of these different readings are we to take as asserted?

On the first reading, the process is partly constituted of (and in this sense is dependent upon) forms of consciousness and intelligent acts. At the same time, to be compatible with M4, these forms of consciousness and acts of intelligence must themselves be determined to be what they are by the laws governing the process of social change. Only if this is so can "social development" proceed according to necessity.

When we turn to M5, however, it appears that the M3A reading of M3 is ineligible. According to M5, any critical inquiry whose intent is to understand and appraise the content and course of civilization itself cannot explain that content and course by appeal to anything that is a form or result of human consciousness. It seems, then, that the more extreme reading M3B is what the reviewer asserts. The alleged law-governed process is one that human consciousness, intelligence, and will not only do not control. They constitute no part of the process.

With these assertions, and Marx's seeming acceptance of them before us, let us first look at some passages written by Marx himself in 1851–52, twenty years before the St. Petersburg review of the yet to be written first volume of *Capital*.

4

In *The Eighteenth Brumaire of Louis Bonaparte*,[5] Marx undertakes to explain the successful overthrow of republican government in France in December 1851 by Louis Bonaparte, Napoleon Bonaparte's (reputed) nephew. (The title of the essay alludes to the date, by the French revolutionary calendar, on which the first Napoleon seized power from the Directory in 1799.)

Marx opens with a short paragraph, the first sentence of which is famous: "Hegel remarks somewhere that all great, world-historical facts and personages occur, as it were twice. He has forgotten to add: the first time as tragedy, the second time as farce."

A second, longer paragraph, begins as follows:

> Men make their own history, but they do not make it just as they please; they do not make it under circumstances chosen by themselves, but under circumstances directly found, given and transmitted from the past. (595)

Note the assertion that it is human beings who make human history. Human actions and practices cause that history to be what it is. Human beings are not, however, able to shape their history exactly as they please. They are confined by circumstances (natural and social) within which, and in relation to which, they must act, but which they have not chosen but inherited. Into these circumstances each is born, and comes to maturity; yet these are not (in most cases) the circumstances, natural or social, that each would have chosen, had it been left to them to make human history "just as they please".

It is obvious that these assertions contradict the St. Petersburg reviewer's remarks. So too, do the sentences that directly follow them:

> The tradition of all the dead generations weighs like a nightmare on the brain of the living. And just when they [who are alive and acting in the present] seem engaged in revolutionising themselves and things, in creating something entirely new, precisely in such epochs of revolutionary crisis [which provoke uncertainty and fear] they anxiously conjure up the spirits of the past to their service and

borrow from them names, battle slogans and costumes in order to present the new [and so uncertain and anxiety-producing] scene of world history in this time-honoured [and so familiar and reassuring] disguise and this borrowed language. Thus Luther donned the mask of the apostle Paul, the [French] Revolution of 1789 to 1814 draped itself alternately as the Roman Republic and the Roman Empire, and the Revolution of 1848 knew nothing better to do than to parody, in turn, 1789 and the revolutionary tradition of 1793 to 1795. In like manner the beginner who has learnt a new language always translates it back into his mother tongue, but he has assimilated the spirit of the new language and can produce *freely* in it [my emphasis] only when he moves in it without remembering the old and forgets in it his ancestral tongue. (595)

Human beings are here described as doing the revolutionizing in history (revolutionizing, notice, that encompasses change in themselves). Emphasis is placed on states of human consciousness, including human emotions in the face of uncertainty, and on the devices by which human beings attempt to deal with uncertainty and to justify, to themselves and others, deliberate change in "themselves and things". Furthermore, the concluding analogy of the passage implies the possibility of human beings escaping the "dead" weight of past tradition and acting "freely" in relation to new projects and possibilities, without being constricted by the need always to "translate" what they are faced with or attempting into meanings "borrowed" from an "ancestral" language, thereby attempting to "present" these possibilities and actions to themselves in a "time-honoured disguise".

Should anyone suppose this an isolated passage from Marx's *Brumaire*, here are two further passages. The first refers to the period from 24 February 1848 ("the overthrow of Louis Philippe") to 4 May 1848 ("the meeting of the Constituent Assembly").

> The February days originally intended an electoral reform, by which the circle of the politically privileged among the possessing class itself was to be widened and the exclusive domination of the aristocracy of finance overthrown. When it came to the actual conflict, however, when the people mounted the barricades, the National Guard maintained a passive attitude, the army offered no serious resistance and the monarchy ran away, the republic appeared to be a matter of course. Every party construed it [the forthcoming republican form of government] in its own sense. Having been won by the proletariat by force of arms, the proletariat impressed its stamp on it and proclaimed it to be a *social republic* [Marx's emphasis]. There was thus indicated the general content [i.e., the representative idea and aspiration] of the modern revolution, which stood in most singular contradiction to everything that, with the material at hand, *with the degree of education attained by the masses*, under the given circumstances *and relationships* [my emphases], could be immediately realized in practice. (600)

84   *Chapter Three*

The second passage that is obviously recalcitrant to the St. Petersburg reviewer's pronouncements occurs two pages later. (In fact, virtually the entire essay is incompatible with the Russian reviewer's remarks, as I shall argue in a moment. What I seek to do here is simply to produce some representative passages in evidence of that.) Italics in the passage are Marx's, except where otherwise noted.

> The defeat of the June [proletarian] insurgents, to be sure, had now prepared and levelled the ground on which the bourgeois [as distinct from social] republic could be founded and built up, but it had shown at the time that in Europe there are other questions involved than that of 'republic or monarchy'. It had revealed that here [in Europe] bourgeois republic signifies the unlimited despotism of one class over other classes. It had proved that in lands with an old *civilization* [my emphasis], with a developed formation of classes, with modern conditions of production, and with an intellectual *consciousness* [my emphasis] into which all traditional ideas have been absorbed by the work of centuries, [the expression] the republic signifies in general only the political form of the revolution of bourgeois society and not its conservative form of life . . . (602)

This passage attributes to France a modern form of production, yet asserts that France is without a corresponding "form of life". The explanation of this fact is said to be that France is a society with "an old civilization" and "an intellectual consciousness" into which all "traditional ideas" have been absorbed. The word 'republic' in these conditions signifies only the introduction of some of the political forms of republican government. It does not signify that the society has ceased to be animated by "centuries" old "conservative" values and "traditional ideas". Having said all of this, Marx goes on, in the essay, to cite as part of the explanation of Louis Napoleon's successful coup his adroit exploitation of the susceptibility of all classes other than the urban Paris proletariat to manipulative appeals to "the watchwords of the old society, 'property, family, religion, order'". This susceptibility enabled "the nephew" to represent even the most superficial liberalization of French society as an "attempt on society" and "socialism".

All of this reasoning is patently incompatible with the St. Petersburg reviewer's *dicta*. It is also, notice, problematic for HM, in its stress upon the enduring and relatively autonomous momentum of "standing (e.g. cultural) circumstances" (to recall Cohen's phrase from *HLF* 27 quoted in Chapter One).

The remaining part of Marx's explanation in the essay of how "a nation of thirty-six millions can be surprised and delivered unresistingly into captivity by three high class swindlers" (599) centers upon two factors: the peasantry who form the majority of French citizens, and the existence of an extensive state bureaucracy and military organization. Marx identifies this organization as having begun under the Bourbon absolute monarchy, been extended by the Revolution, been "perfected" by Napoleon, and been swollen further by the succeeding two monarchies. By 1850, he claims, "the state machine has consolidated its position so thoroughly that the chief of the Society of December [Louis Napoleon] suffices for its head, an adventurer blown in from abroad, elevated on the shield of a drunken soldiery, which he has bought with liquor and sausages, and which he must continually ply with sausage anew" (607). The role of the peasantry in the events under consideration is explained by Marx as proceeding mainly from their passionate fixation upon several "idées napoleoniennes", which obsessively represent to them the return of the prosperity and prestige they believed themselves to enjoy under the first Napoleon. Marx's discussion focuses repeatedly on the peasants' consciousness, on what they want, and what they look to "the nephew" to uphold and provide. In the four decades since the Empire, the economic situation of the French peasantry has been returned to that under the Bourbons, with the difference that now they labour for a bank to which 'their' land is irretrievably mortgaged, where before they laboured for a "seigneur". Yet, Marx stresses, in their political actions a majority of the peasants are governed by their "stupified bondage" to "the ghost of the empire", a triumph of "superstition" and "prejudice" over "enlightenment" and "judgment" which keeps all but a small minority of the peasants from appreciating that their interests actually lie with the urban proletariat (609–11). In the course of identifying those interests, Marx remarks:

> Sixteen million peasants (including women and children) dwell in hovels, a large number of which have but one opening, others only two and the most favoured only three. And windows are to a house what the five senses are to the head. To the four million (including children, etc.) officially recognized paupers, vagabonds, criminals and prostitutes in France must be added five millions who hover on the margin of existence and either have their haunts in the countryside itself or, with rags and their children, continually desert the countryside for the towns and the towns for the countryside. (611)

In the *Eighteenth Brumaire's* stress upon the working of anxieties and images in political events, one is reminded, when reading it, of nothing more than the politics of the Reagan and Bush II eras in the United States. In its sensitivity to the basic needs of human beings, and in its appreciation of the vulnerability to delusion and manipulation that denial of those needs creates, Marx's essay anticipates much that contemporary social theory still insufficiently heeds.

The *Brumaire* has two further features that bear noting. The first is the sense given by the essay to the expression "material conditions". The other is its occasional echo of Hegel.

Mid-way through the closing section of the essay (Section VII), we find this passage. (Emphases are mine.)

> After the first revolution had transformed the peasants from semi-villeins into freeholders, Napoleon [I] confirmed and regulated the conditions on which they could exploit undisturbed the soil of France which had only just come into their possession and slake their youthful passion for property. But what is now [in 1852] causing the ruin of the French peasant is his dwarf holding itself, the division of land, the *form of property* which Napoleon [I] consolidated in France. It is precisely the *material conditions* which had made the feudal peasant into a small peasant and [the first] Napoleon into an Emperor. Two generations have sufficed to produce the inevitable result: progressive deterioration of agriculture, progressive indebtedness of the agriculturist. (610)

We find Marx in these sentences describing as material conditions the property and power relations of feudalism. It is because the pre-revolutionary social mode of agricultural production in France was by "semi-villeins" labouring on small holdings held under direct lease or 'share-cropping' tenantry that the revolutionary settlement of land rights constituted "small peasants" out of "feudal peasants". We also find Marx in these sentences straightforwardly stating that it is the extent of the French peasant's property that is causing his ruin. That "ruin" consisted in an inability to increase or even sustain production to an output sufficient even for minimal subsistence, let alone a rising standard of living. Marx here asserts that the cause of that inability was the "dwarf holding", the extent of land over which each peasant family had rights and effective powers. The "progressive deterioration of agriculture" in France is explained as proceeding from "the division of the land, the form of property which Napoleon consolidated". Property arrangements, in other words, are here held to be a cause of productive decline (presumably in such ways as by causing disoptimal employment of existing agricultural technologies, increased vulnerability to natural destructive forces and market fluctuations, and disinclination or inability to utilise or develop more productive technologies). The property relations of the society are here straightforwardly recognized as a causal factor in economic productivity, with no attempt made to explain these relations as themselves caused by some identified type of productive forces. Rather, the explanation of the specific distribution of property in land that is here said to be causing present productive decline is identified as: the previous property and power relations of feudalism. All of this is incompatible with HM.

The residue of Hegel's social theory in the essay is visible in these two paragraphs (italics by Marx):

> "*C'est le triomphe complet et definit du socialisme!*"
> Thus Guizot characterized December 2 [1851, the date of Louis Bonaparte's coup]. But if the overthrow of the parliamentary republic contains within itself the germ of the triumph of the proletarian revolution, its immediate and obvious result was the victory of Bonaparte over parliament, of *the executive power over the legislative power, of force without phrases over the force of phrases.* . . . France, therefore, seems to have escaped the despotism of a class only to fall back beneath the despotism of an individual, and, what is more, beneath the authority of an individual without authority. The struggle seems to be settled in such a way that all classes, equally impotent and equally mute, fall on their knees before the club.
>
> But the revolution [meaning the *proletarian* revolution] is thoroughgoing. It is still in process of passing through purgatory. It does its work methodically. By December 2, 1851, it had completed one half of its preparatory work; it is now completing the other half. First it perfected the parliamentary power, in order to be able to overthrow it. Now that it has attained this, it perfects the executive power, reduces it to its purest expression, sets it up against itself as the sole target, in order to concentrate all its forces of destruction against it. And when it has done this second half of its preliminary work, Europe will leap from her seat and exultantly exclaim: Well grubbed, old mole! [The reference is to a remark by Hamlet in the first act of Shakespeare's play: "Well said, old mole! Can'st work in the earth so fast?"] (606)

The second of these two paragraphs is nonsense in the style of Hegel, bearing all the marks of the original. Here is the 'world-historical agent' ("the revolution", or more correctly, perhaps, human freedom, of which the revolution will be the realized expression). Here is the dialectical working out of each 'moment' into its purest, most complete form ("perfected the parliamentary power . . . perfects the executive power . . . to its purest expression") in order that each of these succeeding 'theses' may then be opposed by its 'antithesis'. Here is the confident reading off from the 'logic' of the process the next triumphant stage, for which each previous moment is "preparatory" and "preliminary"; and so on. The first paragraph is of a piece with the second, even to its pronouncing Louis Napoleon's coup as "containing within itself the germ of the triumph of the proletarian revolution".

Nor are these the only places in the essay where G.W.F. Hegel looms over the shoulder of the former disciple. The *Eighteenth Brumaire* exhibits throughout an oscillation between Marx still slightly drunk on Hegel and Marx now sober (to adapt Cohen's reference to Marx's "more sober moments" encountered in Chapter One). While the sober Marx commands much of the thought in the essay, the one-time Hegel imbiber keeps breaking out, especially in the expression of the essay, though not only in the expression. An example is this passage in the first section of the essay. (Italics are Marx's.)

88   *Chapter Three*

> The February Revolution was a sudden attack, a taking of the old society by *surprise*, and the people proclaimed this unhoped for *stroke* as a world-historic deed, opening the new epoch. On December 2 the February revolution is conjured away by a card-sharper's trick, and what seems overthrown is no longer the monarchy; it is the liberal concessions that were wrung from it by century-long struggles. Instead of *society* having conquered a new content for itself, the *state* only appears to have returned to its oldest form, to the shamelessly simple domination of the sabre and the cowl. This is the answer to the *coup de main* of February 1848, given by the *coup de tête* of December 1851. Easy come, easy go. (597)

If we interrupt the passage at this point, we appear to have a report of events that are thoroughly contingent and that disclose no progressive or inexorable 'logic'. Certainly, the concluding "easy come, easy go" especially invites this reading, since these words are hardly the language of 'logical necessity'. However, if we continue the passage we are told:

> Meanwhile, the interval has not passed unused. During the years 1848 to 1851 French society has made up, and that by an abbreviated, because revolutionary, method, for the studies and experiences which, in a regular, so to speak, textbook development would have had to precede the February Revolution, if the latter was to be more than a disturbance on the surface. Society now seems to have fallen back behind its point of departure: it has in truth first to create for itself the revolutionary point of departure, the situation, the relationships, the conditions, under which modern revolution alone becomes serious. (597)

Mixed together here are residue of Hegel and active intelligence of Marx. The sentence beginning "Meanwhile" signals that the "easy come, easy go" remark of a moment before was sardonic. If one attends only to how things "seem" or "appear", then history does give the impression, "easy come, easy go". However, we are now supposed to register the fact that below the surface of what may look like completely contingent and erratic—even retrogressive—events, "society" has "conquered a new content for itself'"(recalling a remark of the previous sentences). The interval of 1848 to 1851 "has not", contrary to appearances, "passed by unused". It has been used by "society" to learn the lesson that it has yet to create the circumstances under which revolutionary action by "society" (as opposed to action by some class or ruling officials of society) "alone becomes serious"—that is, has a real probability (Marx doubtless might have said certainty) of succeeding.

The mixture of Hegel-like reasoning with good sense in these sentences is made possible by the endless malleability of language. What Marx has most in mind in observing and commenting upon French events is that even what may *look* like complete and discouraging regress can nevertheless have some good effects. Of course, one wishes that the regressive events had not occurred at all. But, still, their consequence may not be all bad. One good effect even of failure can be increased knowledge of the conditions necessary for probable success. So, even where an attempted revolution fails, the effort has not wholly been without good effect. The process of attempting and being defeated "has not passed by unused" if those who are committed to revolutionary change are alert to what the failed attempt discloses about the conditions of probable success.

All of this is good sense. Furthermore, it is good sense that can be expressed in words that in their surface syntax can also carry a different meaning: such as, that the years 1848–1851 have "not passed by unused" by some world-historical *agent*, "society", whose actions constitute a 'dialectical' process of 'learning' and 'realization' that proceeds, beneath what may *seem* or *appear* to be contingent events, according to a 'logic' discernible to the investigator who can read the truth beneath the surface.

We arrive here at an important fact: that one can mean one thing by a group of words, even as these same words can also express something else one has in mind. This something else that one has in mind one may regard as evidence establishing the truth of what one *expressly intends* the words to express; or one may even regard it as essentially the *same* thought (not recognizing that the two are different). Whichever it is, the meaning for which there is good evidential support may give credence to the meaning for which there is little evidential support. Without being aware of it, one thinks that because this thought is obviously sensible to assert, this other too is obviously sensible to assert, without recognizing that though the same words are being used to express these different assertions, this does not make the assertions equally sensible. Indeed, precisely because each is being expressed in the same words, one is inclined to take them to be the identical thought. In this way a thinker may move back and forth between credible and less credible lines of reasoning and description, without appreciating that he is doing so. He fails to appreciate that the less credible line of thought is trading illegitimately in the currency (if one may so express it) of the more credible propositions.

I submit that the above is a very important fact about human theorizing, and a basic part of the explanation why we find even in Marx's late writings empirically grounded good sense (often of a high order of insight) occasionally tricked out in the language of 'laws', 'necessity', 'inevitability', and figuring such reified agents as 'capital', 'the revolution', 'history', and so on. This phenomenon we shall encounter again and again in Marx's writings, as we proceed to separate within them the explanations and theory he *uses* from the theory he continues, even into the 1870s, to 'talk'. It will be helpful to keep the above fact about language and theorizing in mind as we do so.

90   *Chapter Three*

Two further examples of the phenomenon in the early writings of Marx are the 1848 *Communist Manifesto* and his 1853 essays on India. However, before turning to them it will be helpful to take up briefly the issue of 'necessity' claims, which are one of the repeated elements in the St. Petersburg reviewer's representation of Marx's thought.

5

We have already remarked upon the importance assigned ideas by *The Eighteenth Brumaire*, an importance captured succinctly in Marx's assertion that "The fixed idea of the nephew [to be Emperor of the French] was realised, because it coincided with the fixed idea of the most numerous class of the French people". The primary fixed idea (Marx also refers to it as a "faith") was "that a man named Napoleon would bring all the glory back to them" (608–9). Of all the *idées fixes* of the peasants, Marx comments at one point (emphases are his):

> One sees: all idées napoleoniennes *are the ideas of the undeveloped small holding in the freshness of its youth*: for the small holding that has outlived its day they are an absurdity. They are only the hallucinations of its death struggle, words that are reduced to phrases, spirits reduced to ghosts. But the parody of imperialism [which was Louis Napoleon's 'Empire'] was necessary to free the mass of the French nation from the weight of tradition and to work out in pure form the opposition between the state power and society. With the progressive undermining of this small holding property, . . . the French peasant parts with his belief in his small holding, the entire state edifice erected on this small holding falls to the ground and the *proletarian revolution* obtains *that chorus without which its solo song in all peasant nations becomes a swan song.* (613–14)

Consider the sentence in this passage which asserts that "the parody of imperialism was necessary to free the mass of the French nation" (and so on). This sentence is ambiguous between two very different assertions:

1. *If* the peasant majority of the French nation are to throw off their traditional aspirations and allegiances, and recognize the opposition between the Napoleonic state power and society, *then* some such set of events as Louis Napoleon's seizure of power and rule as Emperor are necessary to bring this about.

2. Louis Napoleon's seizure of power and rule as Emperor *necessarily* will occur, because except they occur the peasant majority of the French nation will not come to throw off their traditional aspirations and allegiances and recognize the opposition between such a "state machine" and society.

The first statement asserts what I shall term *contingent necessity*, of which further examples are:

3. If you wish to be in good health, it is necessary that you eat a nourishing diet.

4. If you wish not to be delayed on a long automobile journey, it is necessary that you ensure that your vehicle has sufficient gasoline before you set out.

5. If you are to pass the examination, it is necessary that you have the minimal knowledge and competence required to produce satisfactory work in the subject.

6. If human beings are to flourish on this planet, it is necessary that they not continually despoil the natural environment.

Each of the five statements (1), and (3) to (6), differs from (2), for the reason that (2) asserts what I shall term *absolute necessity*. Further examples of type (2) statements are:

7. "The hand mill [necessarily] gives you society with the feudal lord, the steam mill [necessarily gives you] society with the industrial capitalist." (*The Poverty of Philosophy*, 1847)

8. "No social order ever perishes before all the productive forces for which there is room in it have developed; and new, higher relations of production never appear before the material conditions of their existence have matured in the womb of the old society itself." (Preface to *A Contribution to a Critique of Political Economy*, 1859)

9. "The basic thought running through the *Manifesto*—that economic production and the structure of society of every historical epoch necessarily arising therefrom constitute the foundation for the political and intellectual history of that epoch . . .—this basic thought belongs solely and exclusively to Marx." (Engels, Preface to the 1883 German edition of *Manifesto of the Communist Party*)

The last of these three statements, notice, is by Engels, but it has an obvious parallel in the first statement, from Marx's 1847 tract against Proudhon.

The words 'necessary', 'necessity', 'inevitable', 'inevitability', pepper Marx's writings. Yet at no point does he appear ever to have sorted out the difference I have marked above by the words 'contingent' and 'absolute' necessity. That difference may be mapped more fully by the following series of contrasts.

10. If human beings are to achieve A, it is necessary that they do B.

11. Human beings necessarily will achieve A, and so they necessarily will do B, causing A to be achieved.

12. If conditions X exist (or come to exist), it is probable that human beings will do Y in order to achieve Z.

13. Conditions X necessarily exist (or necessarily will come to exist), and human beings necessarily will do Y, causing Z necessarily to be achieved.

14. If the human condition under capitalist economic relations is allowed to grow steadily worse for a majority of citizens, it is probable that some at least among these persons will together attempt to overthrow the capitalist social order.

15. The human condition under capitalist economic relations necessarily will grow steadily worse for a majority of citizens, and this majority necessarily will join together to overthrow the capitalist social order.

16. If you are to be in good health, it is necessary that you eat a nourishing diet.

17. You necessarily will be in good health if you eat a nourishing diet, and you necessarily will eat a nourishing diet.

Consider only the last of these statements. The first half of (17) is false. A nourishing diet will not necessarily keep you from a great many (some of them mortal) illnesses. The second half of (17) is also false if it is meant, as here, to assert absolute necessity. Of course, one can employ these same words to attribute contingent necessity. But to do so one must ground the words in an appropriate context, as for example:

18. You are our hostage, and doubtless you wish to continue to live until we release you. We also wish you to continue to live, and despite your own obvious preference for junk food, we control your actions and everything you have access to here, and so you necessarily will eat a nourishing diet during your captivity, and nothing else.

It will be obvious that the distinction between what I have termed absolute and contingent necessity is an important one for any theoretical enterprise whose objective is to explain matters of fact. Failure to distinguish contingent matters from non-contingent matters, and to appreciate correctly which type of circumstance holds in what domains of inquiry, must result in much confusion and error.

Sometimes it is clear that Marx is attributing to actions or events or situations only what I have termed contingent necessity. Sometimes it is not clear whether he means only to attribute contingent necessity. And sometimes it seems that Marx is running together the two kinds of necessity, and means to assert absolute necessity where only contingent necessity could hold. A good example of the first case is this sentence from an *Eighteenth Brumaire* passage already quoted: "Two generations have sufficed to produce the inevitable result: progressive deterioration of agriculture, progressive indebtedness of the agriculturist" (610). This is obviously an assertion of contingent necessity: if agriculture is conducted on dwarf holdings within a society such as France is from 1800 to 1850, it is inevitable that agricultural decline and peasant indebtedness will be the result. (Note that the issue here is not whether Marx's assertion is true, but the kind of 'necessary outcome' he is asserting.) An example of the second, unclear case, is this passage from Marx's and Engels' joint preface to the 1882 Russian edition of the *Communist Manifesto*: "The Communist Manifesto had as its object the proclamation of the inevitably impending dissolution of modern bourgeois property."[6] It is possible to read this as a probability statement, on analogy with, say, 'Her letter had as its object the announcing of the inevitably impending dissolution of her sister's marriage, given that the husband had revealed himself to be an alcoholic wastrel'. But one cannot be as confident here as with the first example, or with such remarks as "State taxes were a necessary means of compulsion to maintain exchange between town and country", again from the *Eighteenth Brumaire* (612).

Part of the reason for one's uncertainty is that where a writer means to assert the absolute necessity of some overall 'macro-level' process alleged to be operating, he or she may, at a more 'micro' level, attribute necessity in language that looks to be asserting only contingent relationships, though in fact the writer intends something more than that.—State taxes necessarily come to be imposed, because they are a necessary means to maintaining exchange between town and country, and such exchange is one requisite 'moment' in the necessary coming to be of a perfected capitalist economy, and so on. Here we have 'necessity' played in two keys, as it were. A passage where we appear to find Marx doing just this (the third case mentioned above) occurs in his preface to the first (the German) edition of Volume One of *Capital*:

> Intrinsically, it is not a question of the higher or lower degree of development of the social antagonisms that result from the natural laws of capitalist production. It is a question of these laws themselves, of these tendencies working with iron necessity towards inevitable results. The country that is more developed industrially only shows, to the less developed, the image of its own future. (90–91)

Is Marx asserting here that if any society develops industrial capitalism then that economic system has a logic (connected to the social decision procedure of a market and production for profit) that will lead necessarily (so long as the society remains capitalist) to certain states of affairs? Or is he asserting that "humanity" (to jump to the higher register) necessarily will develop capitalist economies, and these capitalist economies will pass through a sequence of stages with iron necessity until certain results are reached,—results that are inevitable and unavoidable *even before a fully capitalist economy is reached*?—Hence even societies that are still only in the early stages of industrial capitalism can read their own *inevitable* future in those that are farther advanced?

It will, I hope, now be appreciated that it is important to identify exactly what Marx means to commit himself (and his readers) to when employing in specific sentences the expressions 'necessity', 'necessary', 'inevitable', and their cognates.

6

The relevance of the previous section to the concerns of the present chapter is its bearing on M1 and M2 of the St. Petersburg review. Those two propositions, the reader will recall, are:

M1. The present arrangements of any society exist necessarily. That is, they could not have been otherwise than they are.

M2. It will necessarily come to pass that these present arrangements will be succeeded by a new social order.

Now, in fact, M2 is not quite adequate as a statement of what Marx sometimes asserts. As it stands, all M2 appears to assert is that any human society necessarily will be succeeded by a different kind of social order of some kind or other. However, what Marx not infrequently asserts is that at least some historically existing social forms necessarily will be succeeded by a different social form of a quite specific type. Thus in the *Communist Manifesto*, in the course of a brief discussion of what he terms "Feudal Socialism" (by which he means the political opinions of the French Legitimists and such English conservatives as Carlyle and the young Disraeli), Marx declares:

> In pointing out that their mode of exploitation was different to that of the bourgeoisie, the feudalists forget that they exploited under circumstances and conditions that were quite different, and that are now antiquated. In showing that, under their rule, the modern proletariat never existed, they forget that the modern bourgeoisie is the *necessary* offspring of their own form of society (492, my emphasis).

This is a passage in which we seem to find both kinds of necessity driving the assertion. We appear to have the contingent claim: 'if feudalism, then necessarily bourgeois capitalism afterwards'; a claim that (as I shall show in the next chapter) we have no reason to accept, and which we can already appreciate is not supportable by functional explanation. We also appear to have (when we read the sentences in the context of the entire *Manifesto*) the assertion that the emergence of bourgeois capitalism is a necessary and inevitable stage in human history, "the product of a long course of development, of a series of revolutions in the modes of production and of exchange" (*Manifesto* 475), "the final and most complete expression of the system of producing and appropriating products, that is based on class antagonisms, on the exploitation of the many by the few" (484), which humanity "has to pass through" (484) to reach the "equally inevitable" next stage, the "victory of the proletariat", "the self-conscious, independent movement of the immense majority, in the interests of the immense majority" (482–3). Thus what appears to be the contingent necessity claim, 'if feudalism, then capitalism', at the same time looks to be wrapped in an absolute necessity claim asserting the necessary occurrence of feudalism itself, of its succession by capitalism, of the proletarian revolution, of all that went before these, of all that comes after, in short, the whole scenario.

Yet at the same time, this very essay, the *Communist Manifesto*, seems to exhibit an undeniable recognition that the development of industrial capitalism has to be explained by reference to a great many factors and events, most of them utterly contingent, though some of them admitting of considerable probability *once some of the other things have taken place*. Consider these paragraphs from the second page of the *Manifesto*:

> From the serfs of the Middle Ages [who had fled serfdom to gather in self-defending settlements] sprang the chartered burghers [i.e., chartered by centralizing royal governments] of the earliest towns. From these burgesses the first elements of the bourgeoisie [i.e., town-'bourg'-dwelling persons engaged in production and trade].
>
> The discovery of America, the rounding of the Cape, opened up fresh ground for the rising bourgeoisie. The East-Indian and Chinese markets, the colonisation of America, trade with the colonies, the increase in the means of exchange and in commodities generally, gave to commerce, to navigation, to industry [note the order in which these are mentioned], an impulse never before known, and thereby, to the revolutionary element in the tottering feudal society, a rapid development. [Note that nothing said to this point entails or licenses the conclusion that the reason feudal society was tottering was the presence within it of this revolutionary element, the bourgeoisie, who were revolutionary just in the sense that the interests of a growing number of them

were not best served by continuation of many of the features of feudal government and social organization.]

The feudal system of industry, under which industrial production was monopolized by closed guilds, now no longer sufficed for the growing wants of the new markets. The manufacturing system took its place [i.e., in particular, the rural putting out system of production]. The guild-masters were pushed on one side by the manufacturing middle class; division of labour between the different corporate guilds vanished in the face of division of labour in each single workshop.

Meanwhile, the markets kept ever growing, the demand ever rising. Even manufacture no longer sufficed. *Thereupon* [my emphasis] steam and machinery revolutionised industrial production. The place of manufacture was taken by the giant, Modern Industry, the place of the industrial middle class, by the industrial millionaires, the leaders of whole industrial armies, the modern bourgeoisie.

Modern industry has established the world market, for which the discovery of America paved the way. This market has given an immense development to commerce, to navigation, to communications by land. This development has, in its turn, reacted [note the *feed-back* attribution] on the extension of industry; and in proportion as industry, commerce, navigation, railways extended, in the same proportion the bourgeoisie developed, increased its capital, and pushed into the background every class handed down from the Middle Ages. [These last eight words are worth noting, as we shall have occasion to recall them later in this chapter.]

In these five short paragraphs Marx asserts that among the causes of the development of a capitalist class exercising hegemony over other classes were (1) the repudiation of the social condition of serfdom by individuals who were able to win political support and protection from monarchs seeking to increase their own wealth and to impose their own hegemony on feudal magnates, (2) the coming into being of new markets for goods, as a result of European discovery of other societies and of cost-efficient trade routes to these markets, (3) the inability of merchants and producers to exploit these markets most profitably within the feudal organization of industry and trade, leading to their devising new ways of organizing production that lessened or escaped the constraints of the guild system, (4) the increase in wealth that the exploitation of these new markets and industrial arrangements produced.

From these developments there arose an impetus to develop new technologies, issuing in "steam and machinery" that "revolutionised industrial production" technologically. But the bourgeoisie had *already* revolutionized production earlier in introducing "the manufacturing system", which involved changes in the organization and employment of existing "productive forces", including human labour power. And these changes in the mode of production were themselves spurred by prior, *non-production* developments of discovery, new markets, expanded commerce, improved communications and transport, and so on. In short, this fundamental historical change did not, on

Marx's account here, originate in changes in "productive forces" understood as technology, but in non-production developments and changes in the use of existing technologies.

Throughout this *Manifesto* account no mention is made of the necessity of any of these developments occurring, other than the unexceptional implication that had merchants and producers not developed new ways of organizing production they could not have so profitably exploited the new circumstances, and so on. At the same time, many of the developments are of a kind that are obviously contingent, both as to time and content, as in the case of the Americas being discovered then, a trade route around the Cape being found then, and East Asia being peopled by large populations distinguished by complex civilizations.

Now, as it happens, half a dozen years after Marx and Engels jointly produced the *Communist Manifesto* (the final version of which appears to have been written primarily by Marx), Marx wrote two short essays on British rule in India for *The New York Herald Tribune*[7]. These are of interest both for their diametric opposition, in several places, to the passages from the St. Petersburg *Messenger* under discussion, and also because they provide further examples of the chronic ambiguity of Marx's references to 'history', 'laws of political economy', and so on. A good example of some sentences that contrast sharply with the St. Petersburg review's dicta are these from the first essay on India:

> There have been in Asia, generally, from immemorial times, but three departments of government: that of Finance, or the plunder of the interior; that of War, or the plunder of the exterior; and, finally, the department of Public Works. climate and territorial conditions . . . constituted artifical irrigation by canals and waterworks the basis of Oriental agriculture. . . . This prime necessity of an economical and common use of water, which, in the Occident [Europe] drove private enterprise to voluntary association, as in Flanders and Italy, necessitated, in the Orient where *civilization* was too low [my emphasis] and the territorial extent too vast to call into life voluntary association, the interference of the centralizing power of government. (655)

Here Marx appeals to the state of civilization in India as part of the explanation why "an economical function devolved upon all Asiatic governments" (655). A passage invoking activity by peoples external to India in explanation of India's present state of social life is this one from the same essay:

> All the civil wars, invasions, revolutions, conquests, famines [of the past in India], strangely complex, rapid and destructive as the successive action in Hindoostan may appear, did not go deeper than its surface. England has broken

down the entire framework of Indian society, without any symptoms of reconstitution yet appearing. This loss of his old world, with no gain of a new one, imparts a particular kind of melancholy to the present misery of the Hindoo, and separates Hindoostan, ruled by Britain, from all its ancient traditions, and from the whole of its past history. (654–5)

A further reference to civilization as explanatory of Indian history, past and present, is this passage from the second essay:

> Arabs, Turks, Tartars, Moguls, who had successively overrun India, soon became *Hindooised*, the barbarian conquerors being, by an eternal law of history, conquered themselves by the superior civilization of their subjects. [!] The British were the first conquerors superior, and therefore, inaccessible to Hindoo civilization. They destroyed it by breaking up the native communities, by uprooting the native industry, and by levelling all that was great and elevated in the native society. (659)

Concerning the native communities and the course of Indian society under British rule, Marx offers the following *critique* (recalling deliberately the word from the St. Petersburg review), in which we find an even more explicit appeal to forms of human consciousness, together with an even more explicit repudiation of the St. Petersburg review's denigration of human intelligence and will.

> Now, sickening as it must be to human feeling to witness those myriads of industrious patriarchal and inoffensive social organizations disorganized and dissolved into their units, thrown into a sea of woes, and their individual members losing at the same time their ancient form of civilization, and their hereditary means of subsistence, we must not forget that these idyllic village communities, inoffensive though they may appear, had always been the solid foundation of Oriental despotism, that they restrained the human mind within the smallest possible compass, making it the unresisting tool of superstition, enslaving it beneath traditional rules, depriving it of all grandeur and historical energies. We must not forget the barbarian egotism which, concentrating on some miserable patch of land, had quietly witnessed the ruin of empires, the perpetration of unspeakable cruelties, the massacre of the population of large towns, with no other consideration bestowed upon them than on natural events, itself the helpless prey of any aggressor who had deigned to notice it at all.

It is worth stopping in mid-passage to note the moral considerations appealed to in this appraisal of the traditional "village system" of India, and also the distinction between "natural events" and human events. Marx continues:

> We must not forget that this undignified, stagnatory, and vegetative life, that this passive sort of existence evoked on the other part, in contradistinction, wild,

aimless, unbounded forces of destruction and rendered murder itself a religious rite in Hindoostan. We must not forget that these little communities were contaminated by distinctions of caste and slavery, that they *subjugated man to external circumstances instead of elevating man to be the sovereign of circumstances* [my emphasis], that they transformed a *self-developing* social state into never changing natural destiny [again my emphasis], and thus brought about a brutalising worship of nature, exhibiting its degradation in the fact that man, the sovereign of nature, fell down on his knees in adoration of *Hanuman*, the monkey, and *Sabbala*, the cow. (657–8)

The psychological thesis in these passages concerning the source and role of violence and religious beliefs in Indian society anticipates some of the insights of Nietzsche, while the pronouncement that human beings have the potential to be, and are only alive in a way appropriate to their human nature when they are, "the sovereign of nature", could not be a more emphatic repudiation of the St. Petersburg review's representation of Marx's thought.

At one point in the two essays Marx asks: "Such a country and such a society, were they not the predestined prey of conquest?" (659) It is obvious that what he means here is that if the geophysical and social facts constituting "a country" *are* as they are in India, the society will be vulnerable to continued predation from more coherent and vigorous communities. Because this is the case with India, Marx asserts, the basic question for any inquirer into Indian affairs "is not whether the English had a right to conquer India, but whether we are to prefer India conquered by the Turk, by the Persian, by the Russian, [or by someone else] to India conquered by the Briton." (659) It is this question that Marx addresses in both essays on India, and it is instructive to look at his way of answering it in each. His answer in the first essay is summarized in an often quoted pair of paragraphs with which the first essay concludes.

> England, it is true, in causing a social revolution in Hindoostan, was actuated only by the vilest interests, and was stupid in her manner of enforcing them. But that is not the question. The question is, can mankind fulfill its destiny without a fundamental revolution in the social state of Asia? If not, whatever may have been the crimes of England she was the unconscious tool of history in bringing about that revolution.
>
> Then, whatever bitterness the spectacle of the crumbling of an ancient world may have for our personal feelings, we have the right, in point of history, to exclaim with Goethe [and here Marx gives the German, which I shall give here in an English translation]:
>
> > Should this torture then torment us
> > Since it brings us greater pleasure?
> > Were not through the rule of Timur
> > Souls devoured without measure?

The expressions 'tool of history' and 'in point of history' in this passage have led many readers to construe these sentences as exhibiting Marx reasoning in the mode of Hegel. My own view is that while Marx doubtless felt a resonance with Hegel's mode of thinking when penning this language, that mode of thinking was not forefront in his mind as he penned it. The paragraphs directly follow the long passage just quoted above in which Marx speaks of human beings as "the sovereign of nature", and the content of that long passage suggests a more prosaic sense for these sentences that immediately follow it. The question whether "mankind" (note the communal subject) can "fulfill its destiny" is the question whether human beings can come to be alive in a way that fulfills the potential of human beings for a life marked by "pleasure", dignity, and wellbeing as against "despotism", "superstition", "slavery", "degradation", "murder". The question whether England is "the unconscious tool of history" in her Indian policies is the question whether England's actions will have *unintended good consequences*, such that, judged "in point of history", the overall effects of England's rule in India will be found to be the emergence of a society more productive of human good than that Indian society which she has "with the vilest of interests" destroyed.

The importance of unintended consequences in human life is (as we shall see) a basic tenet of Marx's understanding of human history. We find it explicitly invoked in the second of the two essays on India, where Marx discusses at length the probable *but unintended* effect on India of British economic exploitation and political domination of the country. He observes at one point:

> The ruling classes of Great Britain have had, till now, but an accidental, transitory and exceptional interest in the progress of India. The aristocracy wanted to conquer it, the moneyocracy to plunder it, the [textile] millocracy to undersell it. But now the tables have turned. The millocracy have discovered that the transformation of India into a reproductive country has become of vital importance to them, and that, to that end, it is necessary, above all, to gift her with means of irrigation and of internal communication. They intend now drawing a net of railways over India. And they will do it. The results must be inappreciable. (660)

This theme of the unintended contribution of British actions to progress in India is continued two pages later.

> I know that the English millocracy intend to endow India with railways with the exclusive view of extracting at diminished expenses the cotton and other raw materials for their manufactures. But when you have once introduced machinery into the locomotion of a country, which possesses iron and coals, you are un-

able to withold it from its fabrication. You cannot maintain a net of railways over an immense country without introducing all those industrial processes necessary to meet the immediate and current wants of railway locomotion, and out of which there must grow the application of machinery to those branches of industry not immediately connected with railways. . . .

All the English bourgeoisie may be forced to do [in pursuit of its initial intentions, and afterwards despite its initial intentions] will neither emancipate nor materially mend the social condition of the mass of the people, [this last] depending not only on the development of the productive powers, but on their appropriation by the people. But what they will not fail to do is to lay down the material premises for both. Has the bourgeoisie ever done more? Has it ever effected a progress without dragging individuals and peoples through blood and dirt, through misery and degradation? (662)

The reference to blood and dirt we shall find repeated *verbatim* in the first volume of *Capital*. For the moment, note the contingency of all these claims, and the repeated stress on unintended outcomes. Even the 'unable's, 'cannot's and 'must's register instrumental relationships grounding probability claims. — Once do this, and you will find that practical considerations make it unavoidable that you also do this other thing, and probable and unpreventable that others will do something more (and so on).

The same is true of other predictions in the essay, such as this one (that comes just before the above passage quoted from page 662): "Modern industry, resulting from the railway-system, will dissolve the hereditary divisions of labour, upon which rest the Indian castes, those decisive impediments to Indian progress and power." (662) The (by us) known falsehood of this confident prediction does not belie the fact that the remark reads most straightforwardly as a probability claim.

Doubtless the remark could intend more than that. Its ambiguity is not disputed. The same kind of ambiguity is discernible in the concluding paragraph of this second of the two essays on India. Referring once more to the "devastating effects of English industry" on India, Marx asserts that

> . . . we must not forget that they are only the organic results of the whole system of production as it is now constituted. That production rests on the supreme rule of capital. The centralisation of capital is essential to the existence of capital as an independent power. The destructive influence of that centralisation upon the markets of the world does but reveal, in the most gigantic dimensions, the inherent organic laws of political economy now at work in every civilised town. (663)

These first sentences of this concluding paragraph continue the now familiar ambiguity. The system of production *as it is now* constituted, the "organic laws" *now at work*, can be read as meaning only that, given that this system of production has come to exist, the noted features are unavoidable consequences. Yet these same words are compatible with a conviction that this system necessarily had to appear, and that the relations and developments referred to obtain with absolute necessity.

Nor are things helped by the next sentence in the paragraph.

> The bourgeois period of history has to create the material basis of the new world—on the one hand the universal intercourse founded upon mutual dependency of mankind, and the means of that intercourse; on the other hand the development of the productive powers of man and the transformation of material production into a scientific domination of natural agencies. (663–4)

It is perhaps worth noting (since the words are directly before us) Marx's reference to "a scientific domination of natural agencies": a way of speaking about the relation of human beings to nature that shows little, if any, sensitivity to the need scrupulously to respect the ecology of the planet and the claims of other life forms. These words are representative of the reasons why Marx is not a favoured figure among those who are struggling to reverse the human record of reckless and unheeding despoilation of the environment. (Yet as we shall see in Chapter Four, Marx shows, in some passages, a keen awareness of the ecological toll of the capitalist mode of production.) For our present purposes, however, the most notable words in the sentence are *"has to create"*, which are ambiguous between:

1. If the material basis of a new world is to be created, it has to be created by the bourgeoisie or it will never be created.

2. The material basis of a new world necessarily will be created, and the bourgeoisie necessarily will come to dominate through "the supreme rule of capital", and necessarily will create the material conditions of that new world.

Taking Marx's sentence as it stands, and out of context, Marx's language may be thought to invite the second construction. Yet consider what comes directly after it, with which the essay concludes. (My emphases.)

> Bourgeois industry and commerce create these material conditions of a new world in the same way *as geological revolutions have created the surface of the earth*. When a great social revolution *shall have* mastered the results of the bourgeois epoch, the market of the world and the modern powers of production, and subjected them to the common control of the most advanced [*sic*] peoples, *then only* will human progress cease to resemble that hideous pagan idol, who would not drink the nectar but from the skulls of the slain.

It is, I think, undeniable that the burden of these two sentences is to assert once again that the contribution capitalist industrialization makes to human progress is unintended by the agents involved, *just as* the shape given the face of the earth by geological revolutions is unintended by any agent or agents. Yet it is striking that the analogy Marx reaches for is to a process—geological reshaping of the earth's surface—that is paradigmatically one of *contingent* events. It is also striking that the way he frames the last sentence is the mode most appropriate to contingent necessity: only when (and if) a great social revolution shall have accomplished the things specified, will human progress cease to resemble the barbaric sacrifice noted.

Still, there is no denying that these two essays on India, as much as they contradict several of the *dicta* iterated by the St. Petersburg review, also leave unresolved the question whether Marx explains 'epochal' social change as occurring contingently or with some kind of non-contingent necessity. The essays at several places admit of being read either way.

That their language does frequently admit of both readings supports my claim that because sentences which can be used to express a defensible contingent claim can also be used to express an indefensible necessity claim, Marx is able to move back and forth between the two kinds of conception and proposition unawares.

The St. Petersburg reviewer (were he around to do so), and also most contemporary commentators on Marx, may object that however ambivalent Marx's earlier writings may reveal him to be on this issue, by 1859 he had rid himself of any ambivalence, as shown by the most explicit statement of his theory he ever produced: the famous, much quoted preface to *A Contribution to the Critique of Political Economy*.

To weigh this objection, we must turn to that preface.

7

The *Contribution to the Critique of Political Economy* was first published in 1859.[8] In his preface to this work Marx gives a brief account of his activities up until that time, and especially for the period 1842 to 1849. We have already had reason to recall his report there that it was in 1842 that he first began "to take part in discussions on so-called material interests" (see section 2 above). Directly after reporting this, Marx informs us that, partly in response to those discussions, he began "a critical review of the Hegelian philosophy of right, a work the introduction to which appeared in 1844". Marx then declares that one result of that (never completed) review was his concluding that "legal relations as well as forms of state . . . have their roots in the material conditions of life", whose "sum total" is what Hegel termed "civil society", and whose "anatomy . . . is to be sought in political economy" (4). (Note again the employment by Marx of the expression "material conditions of life" to encompass the *social* mode of production.) Marx then reports:

> The investigation of the latter [i.e., of political economy], which I began in Paris, I continued in Brussels, whither I had emigrated in consequence of an expulsion order of M. Guizot. The general result at which I arrived, and which won, served as a guiding thread for my studies, can be briefly formulated as follows: . . . (4)

We are then given the well-known sentences to which we shall attend in a moment. First I wish to call attention to three things: (1) that the "general result" is one arrived at from studies began in Paris and "continued in Brussels"; (2) that this "result" is, therefore, one reached by inquiries extending from 1843 to 1849 (at the latest), when Marx moved to London; (3) that this "result" is said to have "served as a guiding thread" to Marx's studies from that time (1849 or earlier) up until 1859, the date of publication of the *Critique*. In other words, the "general result" to which we are about to attend predates much of the investigation and writing that culminated in the first volume of *Capital*.

This is important, since it requires us to be alert to the possibility that this "general result" is one prematurely arrived at, and one not borne out by the intensive and deeply considered studies of the years following 1849, during which Marx was at the height of his intellectual powers. We must also be alert to the possibility that an investigator who reaches such a result relatively early—and reaches it in continued collaboration with another inquirer (Engels) and during active political association with many others (the Communist League and, later, the First International)—may be disposed against recognizing any upset to this position required by later results.

There is a fourth thing to which I wish to call attention before turning to the Preface itself. This is that the sentences we are about to examine *are* a *preface*. They are not Marx *at work*. They are Marx (once more) *talking about* his work, and recounting to us its onetime "general result" and alleged "guiding thread".

What is that "general result"? Marx's answer consists of about a page of text, and I propose to examine the passage a few sentences at a time. Throughout, all italics are mine, as well as all interpolations in square brackets added to clarify Marx's meaning.

Marx begins with two broad claims:

> In the *social* production of their life, men [that is, human beings living together in a human society] enter into definite [social] relations that are indispensible

and independent of their will, [social] relations of production that correspond to a definite stage of development of their material productive forces. The sum total of these relations of production constitutes the economic structure of society, the real foundation on which rises a legal and political superstructure and to which [economic structure there] correspond definite forms of social consciousness.

Note first the generality of these claims, alleged to hold for any human society—for "men", in whatever time or place. Note, secondly, the ambiguity in the first of the two claims of the expression "indispensible and independent of their will". Is Marx asserting that *some* kind of social relations of production appropriately suited to available knowledge and technology are indispensible to any human society? Or is he asserting that a quite specific type of social relations of production is indispensible to a quite specific type of productive forces? By asserting that human beings "enter into definite social relations" that are "independent of their will" does Marx mean only that every human being is born into a society in which there already exist quite particular social relations of production which confront each person as a given and about which none is asked whether he or she wants these social relations or some alternative set? Or does Marx mean as well that these relations of production are independent of anyone's will in the sense that there is no getting along without *some kind* of such relations? Or—does he mean that the existence of such social relations does not *involve* human 'will': does not involve human judgment, agreement, acquiescence?

Regarding the second of the two quoted claims, it will, I hope, be clear from our discussion of "base" and "basic" how ambiguous (and to that extent vacuous) the "real foundation" claim, and the earlier "have their roots in" claim, are. What is also worth noticing, however, is Marx's assertion that "definite forms of social consciousness" correspond to definite types of relations of production or economic structure. This might be thought to imply that what persons conceive to be economic opportunities and useful knowledge is social-structurally sensitive (as indeed we have seen to be the case in looking briefly at China, Islam, and medieval Europe). Yet Marx goes on to assert what looks like a one-way relation:

> The mode of production of material life conditions the social, political and intellectual life process in general. It is not the consciousness of men that determines their being, but, on the contrary, their social being determines their consciousness.

Note again the extreme generality of the claims, combined with pervasive ambiguity as to their content. The allegation "conditions'" is hardly precise, and may mean anything from influences to wholly determines. The words "social . . . and intellectual life process in general" are also exceedingly vague. The reference to the "social" life process could mean anything from production activities and production relations only, to familial, sexual, religious, and other kinds of cultural practices and relationships. The expression "intellectual life process in general" could encompass everything from beliefs or explanations of a very ordinary kind through to science and theoretical activities of a very recondite type.

In addition to their ambiguity and vagueness, there is a *polemical* dimension to these remarks that bears attention. It is expressly signalled by Marx's reporting, a few sentences before, that he reached this "general result" in the course of critically appraising Hegel's *Philosophy of Right* (a major book by a figure whose metaphysical and social theories had for more than a generation dominated the intellectual community that was Marx's immediate audience). Marx expressly states that it was his critical appraisal of Hegel's political theory that led him to "the result that legal relations and forms of state are to be grasped neither from themselves nor from the so-called general development of the human mind, but rather have their roots in the material conditions of life". My own view is that the famous (or notorious) "consciousness/social being" remark is precisely the sort of extreme, one-sided declaration that polemical opposition invites.—"All right! Which is it? Does consciousness determine being? Or does social being determine consciousness? Yes or no? Let's have it!"—"It is not consciousness that determines social being, but social being that determines consciousness."

This famous *dictum* is also the kind of polarised remark that one can hardly keep from sliding into if one undertakes to produce a *general* statement or "result" regarding matters which are extremely complicated and many-sided. That they are complicated and many-sided one may know to be so, and may exhibit that knowledge in one's actual practice. But that knowledge here gets elbowed aside (or deserts one) *just because one has embarked on producing a brief general statement about matters that it is extremely difficult (if not impossible) to reduce to a brief 'general' statement*. This is one of those cases in human life (of which there are many) in which wisdom lies in refraining from the undertaking. Once you, for whatever reason, start in upon it, the probability of a lamentable outcome is exceedingly high. (Indeed, one might say that the proof that your knowledge of the matter has deserted you, in such an instance, is the fact that you have embarked upon the undertaking.)

In any case, Marx, having dispatched the consciousness/being problem in two sentences, then informs us that, in all human societies (there is not, notice, a whisper of qualification to specific types of society or historical period) the following is true:

At a certain stage of their development, the material productive forces of society come in[to] conflict with the existing relations of production, or—what is but a legal expression for the same thing—with the property relations within which they have been at work hitherto. From forms of development of the productive forces these relations turn into their fetters. Then begins an epoch of social revolution. With the change of the economic foundation the entire immense superstructure is more or less rapidly transformed. In considering such transformations a distinction should always be made between the material transformation of the economic conditions of production, which can be determined with the precision of natural science, and the legal, political, religious, aesthetic or philosophic—in short, ideological forms in which men become conscious of this conflict and fight it out. Just as our opinion of an individual is not based on what he thinks of himself, so can we not judge of such a period of transformation by its own consciousness; on the contrary, this consciousness must be explained rather from the contradictions of material life, from the existing conflict between the social productive forces and the relations of production.

The first thing to notice about this scenario is the sharp distinction Marx seeks to draw between "the material transformation of the economic conditions of production" and the "legal, political, religious, aesthetic or philosophic" forms through which the conflict is apprehended and fought out. This distinction tends to disguise the fact that this "material" *transformation* must from its beginnings involve social relations, in the sense of effective powers possessed by some persons in relation to other members of the society (even if these effective powers are not recognized as legal rights). One reason why this must be so is that those persons whose interests are advanced by the new productive forces are not going to be able successfully to fight the issue out except they have economic power deriving from these forces' present use. Another reason is that one can hardly determine "with the precision of natural science" what is not yet being employed, but constitutes only a potential, un-deployed capability. A third reason is Marx's own reference to these productive forces as conflicting with the existing relations of production *"within which they have been at work hitherto"*. Once we appreciate that the material transformation involves social relations respecting the new forces, we see that achievement of such social relations by those persons whose interest it is to exploit these forces is one of the causes of the "social revolution" that comprises "change of the *economic foundation*" of the society.

A second thing observable in the passage is a *non sequitur* in Marx's remarks about consciousness. Even if we grant that we cannot judge what the true explanation (or value?) "of such a period of transformation" is *solely* "from its [i.e., contemporaries'] own consciousness" of that transformation, it does not follow that that consciousness must be wrong. It is entirely possible that (supposing for a moment this conflict were the true explanation) the consciousness of at least some contemporaries is focused on "the existing conflict between the social productive forces and the relations of production". What we encounter here is another trajectory of Marx's earlier tying of forms of consciousness to *extant, dominant* social relations of production. Once you do this, you are bound logically to think that "such a period['s] . . . own consciousness" cannot correctly "correspond" to the truth about the transformation in process. Yet *some* persons' consciousness must correspond to *some* of the truth about the conflict productive of this "fight", or nobody can successfully pursue just that "transformation" of features of the society's common life that constitutes the removal of "contradictions" and the promotion of "development".

A third feature of the passage deserving comment is Marx's reference to "the contradictions of *material* life". This phrase (right in the middle of *the* 'canonical text' of 'Marxism') is troublesome for historical materialism, for the simple reason that the expression 'material life' here encompasses both material facts *and social facts*. As Marx goes on directly to spell out, the "contradiction" consists of "the existing conflict between the social productive forces *and the relations of production*". The unhappiness for HM of this description 'material life' is further compounded by the fact that Marx counts among productive forces ways of organizing productive activity (usually termed by him 'division of labour'). But changes in division of labour most often are both caused by, and consist of, power relations between persons. It was the merchant entrepreneurs who imposed the factory organization of manufacture on producers who before had worked in their own dwellings, often on their own looms, and at their own pace. The introduction of *factory* manufacture was a dramatic increase in productive power. Yet to specify the constitution of productive activity in a factory inextricably "entails ascription to . . . persons of rights or effective powers *vis-à-vis* other persons" (*HLF* 83).

Concerning productive forces, Marx now proceeds to declare:

> No social order ever perishes before all the productive forces for which there is room in it have developed; and new, higher relations of production never appear before the material conditions of their existence have matured in the womb of the old society itself. Therefore mankind only sets itself such tasks as it can solve; since, looking at the matter more closely, it will always be found that the task itself arises only when the material conditions for its solution already exist or are at least in the process of formation.

What is asserted by the first clause of the first sentence of this passage was known to be false even in Marx's time. (One has only to think of the civilizations of Greece, Rome, Egypt, Peru, and Mexico.) The second half of the first sentence contracts the sense of 'material' from that of the sentences just before (now excluding "relations" from "material life"). If we construe the word 'material' in the sense of those previous sentences, the assertion becomes a tautology. But if we construe it in the narrower sense of this passage, *and* at the same time mean by "relations of production" (as Marx does) the "property relations within which" productive forces are employed, then the assertion becomes a truism. Presumably, "higher" relations of production are those appropriate to more productive forces of production, in which case it is uncontentious that such relations will only exist if there have been developed (to operational capacity) forces for which they are the appropriate, "higher" form. (Marx could hardly mean by "higher relations" here, "higher" in some moral sense, since his writings resound with his judgment that capitalist economic relations were much more ruthlessly unheedful of the needs and claims of human beings than most pre-capitalist economic relations.)

We note too the deft descent from "already exist" to "or are at least in the process of formation", a qualification (if one may call it that) which makes nonsense of the assertion that no group or human society (so construing, for a moment, the phrase "mankind") ever undertakes the task of revolutionising the economic foundation of a society unless it can do so—can "solve" the problem. Marx's own *Eighteenth Brumaire*, to cite only one of his writings, written a half dozen years before, flatly contradicts this allegation.

But, of course, what controls Marx's reasoning in these sentences (and defeats his own considerable historical knowledge) is the *supra-individual subject* "mankind", which "sets itself . . . tasks", and in the "womb" of whose successive social forms material conditions "develop" and "mature" that are each a "higher" stage in the progress of "mankind" to an eventual condition of abundance and amity. All of this is, of course, basically the "rational adaptive practices" view, bonded together with something toward which Marx shows a decided inclination: his tendency, when abstractly theorizing or summarizing, to conceive of society on analogy with *organisms*.

This tendency deserves separate consideration, but before undertaking it I wish to end this section by remarking that the 1859 *Critique* preface does not, on inspection, reveal Marx as having by 1859 freed himself of ambivalence or confusion about whether fundamental social change occurs contingently or through some process governed by absolute necessity. To the extent that the preface explicitly invokes states or processes "indispensable and independent" of human "will" it does so ambiguously. Other of its remarks are problematic in other ways, and a few seem even inconsistent with Marx's own categories or with positions attributed to Marx by historical materialism. It is true that some of Marx's language in the 1859 preface suggests a process that is inexorable, not least the sentences last examined, with their talk of mankind always setting itself such tasks as it can solve, "since . . . *it will always be found* that the task itself arises" only when what is necessary to accomplish it lies at hand. The same may be said for the sentences with which Marx's statement of his "general result" and "guiding thread" ends:

> In broad outlines Asiatic, ancient, feudal, and modern bourgeois modes of production can be designated as progressive epochs in the economic formation of society. The bourgeois relations of production are the *last* [my emphasis] antagonistic form of the social process of production—antagonistic not in the sense of individual antagonism, but of one arising from the social conditions of life of the individuals; at the same time the productive forces developing in the womb of bourgeois society create the material conditions for the solution of that antagonism. This social formation brings, therefore, the prehistory of human society to a close. (5)

These sentences do not read like someone waiting upon contingent (and uncertain) developments. All I would observe, by way of concluding comment, is that, taken together, these famous sentences from the 1859 preface fall significantly short of a lucid, coherent explanatory schema for application to major social change. They therefore fail conclusively to show Marx in 1859 lacking ambivalence or confusion about the issue of contingency *versus* necessity, and much else. They also betray a fondness on Marx's part for thinking of social change on analogy with biological processes: wombs, maturings, *pre*histories, and so on. This last issue bears investigation, and in pursuing it we shall return to where we started: the St. Petersburg review of the first volume of *Capital*.

8

When quoting earlier from Marx's 1873 "Afterword", I remarked that the passage reproduced there by Marx from the 1872 review of his book in the St. Petersburg *European Messenger* is a lengthy one. Indeed, the sentences with which we began our discussion are only a part of what Marx quotes from the review. I wish now to look at the remaining sentences (or the bulk of them).

These sentences, remember, are from a review that, according to Marx, "pictures" what the reviewer "takes to be my own actual method, in a striking and, as far as concerns my own application of it, generous way" (102). The reasons for looking at these further sentences are threefold. In the first place, Marx tells us that the St. Petersburg reviewer begins his appraisal of Marx's "method of inquiry" (that part of the review already considered) by first quoting the sentences from the 1859 preface to the *Critique* that we have just examined (100). There is thus a direct connection between that canonical passage and those sentences from the review with which we began and those we shall now examine. A second reason for looking at these further sentences from the St. Petersburg review is that they also make reference to organisms and organic development, and do so more fully than the preface to the *Critique*. The third reason for considering them is that there is, as we shall discover, a curious inconsistency between these further sentences from the review and those with which we started.

We take up the review again at the point where Professor Kaufman attributes to Marx the position that a critique whose object is civilization itself "cannot have for its basis any form or any result of consciousness" (101). In discussing this claim earlier, we focused on its seeming connection to what the reviewer had said immediately before: that Marx allegedly holds that what causes an existing social order to pass over into another social order is a law-governed process that is independent of human will, consciousness, and intelligence (which are themselves allegedly determined by the law-governed process causing social change). However, it is possible (though it would be a rash reader who declared confidently) that the reviewer actually intended this remark about a critique of civilization to be explicated more by reference to these sentences that follow almost directly after:

> This means that it is not the idea but only its external manifestation which can serve as the starting point. A critique of this kind will confine itself to the confrontation and comparison of a fact, not with ideas, but with another fact. The only things of importance for this inquiry is that the facts be investigated as accurately as possible, and that they actually form different aspects of a development *vis-à-vis* each other. But most important of all is the precise analysis of the series of successions, of the sequences and links within which the different stages of development present themselves. (101)

Notice that the first of these four sentences, which may be thought to be spelling out what the remark about a critique of civilization "means", in fact contradicts it. Surely the "*external manifestation*" of an idea is a "*form or . . . result of consciousness*"? Surely, also, the emphasis on grounding one's "critique" on facts does not disqualify ideas, since among the facts relevant to one's inquiry may be the fact that people hold and act upon certain ideas? (Recall the *Eighteenth Brumaire*.) For our present purposes, however, the most important feature of the just-quoted passage is the claim that the facts in need of attention are those comprising aspects of a "development", and the assertion that it is the successive stages of this development that especially require analysis.

The reviewer now anticipates an objection:

> It will be said, against this, that the general laws of economic life are one and the same, no matter whether they are applied to the present or the past. But this is exactly what Marx denies. According to him, such abstract laws do not exist. On the contrary, in his opinion, every historical period possesses its own laws ... As soon as life has passed through a given period of development, and is passing over from one given stage to another, it begins to be subject also to other laws. (101)

These are curious remarks. If every historical period possesses its *own* "laws" of "development", in what sense exactly are these describable as "laws"? The idea of *lawgoverned* social development would seem to imply "laws" that operate transitively *across successive social forms*, and which are describable as *laws* just because they hold of anything that is a form of human society (as Marx's pronouncements in the *Critique* about the relation of productive forces, economic structure, and forms of consciousness expressly suggest).

If the alleged law-governed process is internal to each "historical period" or "epochal" social form, how could one allege a law-governed "social movement" across the course of human history culminating in socialism? If each successive social form has its own laws, how can the series of succeeding forms be connected in a "law-governed" way? How (to recall the reviewer's own earlier language) is one able to assert not only "the necessity of the present order of things" but also "the necessity of another order *into which the first must inevitably pass over*" (my emphasis)?

One is led to suspect that the reviewer is confusing different laws with different results of the operation of the same law in different circumstances. The next group of sentences in the passage confirms this suspicion.

> In short, economic life offers us a phenomenon analogous to the history of evolution in other branches of biology. . . . The old economists misunderstood the nature of economic laws when they likened them to the laws of physics and chemistry. A more thorough analysis of phenomena shows that social organisms differ among themselves as fundamentally as plants or animals. Indeed, one and the same phenomenon falls under quite different laws in consequence of the different general structure of these organisms, the variations of their individual organs, and different conditions in which those organs function. Marx denies, for example, that the law of population is the same at all times and in all places. He asserts, on the contrary, that every stage of development has its own law of population . . . (101–2)

The reviewer contrasts the "laws" governing economic and social change with those governing physical and chemical processes, and claims that the former are analogous to those operating in the historical evolution of plants and animals. He even speaks explicitly of human societies as "social organisms". This conception of human societies I wish to let pass for a moment, and attend only to the way in which the reviewer reasons by analogy with biology to conclusions about organisms of this "social" kind. In the course of this reasoning the reviewer appears to confuse a difference in organic structure and environment with a difference in the laws to which organisms are subject. Because organisms are anatomically different it does not follow that they are subject to different law-like processes. The impact of gravity and heat irradiation on a fly and a shrew, respectively, are different from what they are on a great ape and a dinosaur. But that does not make it the case that the forces and processes to which each is subject here are different. Thus the conclusions drawn analogically about "social organisms" are wholly spurious. The reviewer is on firmer ground in alleging that Marx posits different "laws of population" holding at different times and places. Marx holds that human populations grow or decline at different rates, and with different effects, according to their social and environmental circumstances. There is no "law" of population holding for every human group regardless of circumstance. There are different dynamics of growth, decline and stability, and different effects of these, according to the complex configuration of facts constituting different societies' modes of social life, physical environments, and interactions. What is odd about this position is that Marx expresses it in the language of 'laws', declaring that . . .

> every particular historical mode of production has its own special laws of population, which are historically valid within that particular sphere. An abstract law of population exists only for plants and animals, and even then only in the absence of any historical intervention by man. (784)

Ignoring Marx's questionable claim about plants and animals, this passage exhibits a tension between recognition of greatly variable processes and effects and a wish to capture these in the language of law-like generality. Yet the burden of Marx's words is to repudiate the idea of a "law of population". This does not mean (reverting to the St. Petersburg reviewer's discussion of organisms) that some life forms cannot be affected by forces and processes that others are not affected by (as some organisms are affected by magnetic fields and others are not). What it means is that the same force or process operating upon different types of organism existing in different environments may issue in different effects. But this does not make the forces or processes different.

What could explain the reviewer's falling into this confusion? My guess is that a part of the explanation is the reviewer's misunderstanding of Darwin's theory of evolution. (*The Origin of Species*, remember, had appeared a dozen years before.) A second cause of the reviewer's confusion, I suspect, is a mistake he makes in reading Marx's account in *Capital* of the rise of capitalism in Europe and Marx's arguments about capitalism's decline. As we shall see in detail in the next chapter, in treating these, Marx stresses specific features of the internal economic and social structure of feudal and capitalist societies, and certain unintended contradictions and disintegrative consequences proceeding from those features. The reviewer seems to be confusing Marx's judgment that certain past social forms *had internal features productive of disintegration* with Marx's asserting that each successive social form "has laws of its own". I cannot substantiate this suspicion fully here, which would require the examination of the historical sections of *Capital* to be undertaken in the next chapter. All I can do for the moment is point to two things. One is the reviewer's fixing upon alleged processes of change unique to each "historical period". I submit that the reviewer is mistaking Marx's close attention to specific features of a society and their effects for an attribution by Marx of "special laws" regulating each specific social form. What (as we shall see in the next chapter) is Marx's sensitivity to contingent and unique features of social forms is here mistakenly interpreted as explanation by him in terms of necessary laws, but laws that are "special" to each social form. This mistaken interpretation is paralleled (and buttressed) by the reviewer's confusing of different outcomes with the presence of different "laws".

Linked to these confusions is the reviewer's conceiving of human societies on analogy with biological organisms. This conception carries confusions of an even more basic kind. Recall the question posed a moment ago: how, if each society "has its own laws", can the law-like development of one society be supposed to issue necessarily in another society? The next (and last) sentences quoted by Marx from the St. Petersburg review return us to this issue:

> With the varying degree of development of productive power, social conditions and the laws governing them vary too. While Marx sets himself the task of following and explaining the capitalist economic order from this point of view, he is only formulating, in strictly scientific manner, the aim that every accurate investigation into economic life must have. . . . The scientific value of such an inquiry lies in the illumination of the special laws that regulate the origin, existence, development, and death of a given social organism and its replacement by another, higher one. And in fact this is the value of Marx's book. (102)

Here again we have talk of societies as organisms—talk evocative both of Marx's reference in the *Critique* to "wombs", and, more immediately, of something he says in his preface to the first edition of Volume One of *Capital* (to which the reviewer is doubtless responding) where Marx refers to modern industrial society as "an organism capable of change, and constantly engaged in a process of change" (93). Leaving Marx aside for a moment, and concentrating on the St. Petersburg review sentences in front of us, the reviewer seems not to be aware (despite his parading of the expressions "scientific" and "laws"), that natural organisms do not, at death, undergo transformation into another form of "higher" organism. They do not (shifting to the reviewer's earlier remarks) "inevitably " or otherwise, "pass over" from "one form into another". Organisms inhabiting an environment may eventually, for any number of reasons (some of which we shall look at shortly), become extinct, and may be replaced in that environment by some other type or types of organism. But this is a far cry from "their transition from *one* form *into* another" form of organism, according to some "law of their variation". In the second place, to talk of societies as organisms conflates the biological with the social, a basic error. Some organisms live in relation to their own kind in ways that constitute a social life. But this does not make of their society a 'supra'-organism, or the processes constituting organisms those constituting society. This fact is one that needs emphasis, since it has far-reaching implications for any attribution to human societies of an 'evolution' over time. These attributions, which in the later decades of the nineteenth century were rampant under the rubric "social Darwinism", must always be greeted with extreme caution for two reasons, both relevant to a consideration of Marx's discussions of social change.

The first reason is that where there is evolution of species, there is not, *eo ipso*, social evolution. To suppose so is greatly to misunderstand the processes identified by Darwin in the *Origin*. The natural selection processes that Darwin identified do not operate by means of social processes, but at the level of reproductive biology, and they hold for organisms as variable as bacteria, wildebeest, and professors of economics. Most organisms of which evolution can be predicated have nothing even vaguely approaching intelligence, let alone a social life analogous to human society. It is now common to assert that human societies exhibit a kind of neo-Lamarckian evolution, in that human beings do hand on achieved capabilities to succeeding generations through such social transactions as education and institutional structures. But this is not evolution of the kind that all species exhibit.

The second reason for treating warily attributions of evolution to human societies is because evolution of species (from which the analogy is drawn) is not, contrary to much popular belief, either a *necessary*, or a *progressive*, development. To begin, the existence of species is a proved contingent fact. Indeed, there is now reason to judge that the existence of human beings, in particular, is a colossal piece of luck, hinging on the survival, through successive and frequent massive extinctions of species, of a little-known two-inch long

Cambrian chordate and its descendants named for a mountain a few hundred miles from where these sentences are written (where the first fossil remains of *Pikaia* were found). Secondly, there is no longer any reason to hold (except from a base-line of anthropomorphic preference) that species who survived the successive decimations of life-forms of which we now have knowledge were 'better' forms of life than those extinguished, or that biological history constitutes a 'progress' of life from 'lower' to 'higher' forms. (For the evidence and arguments here see, for example, Stephen Jay Gould's wonderful book *Wonderful Life: The Burgess Shale and the Nature of History*.[9])

Marx conceived of the evolution of species as most persons in the 19th and 20th centuries have—as a progressive development along a linear trajectory from one type of original organism. From this conception he proceeded to conceive of "human" development as an "evolution" through time in a manner analogous to "species" development. In the preface to the first edition of *Capital* Marx speaks of "the development of the economic formation of society" as "a process of natural history"—a "standpoint" (Marx's own word) reported almost *verbatim* by the St. Petersburg reviewer in his remark that "Marx treats the social movement as a process of natural history" (92, 101). We have seen, how, in the same preface, Marx speaks of "the present society" as "an organism capable of change, and constantly engaged in a process of change" (93). I shall argue in the next chapter that Marx's much discussed concept of the "dialectic" is partly connected to his mistakes about biological change. The "dialectic" confuses *intelligibility* with *inevitability*, and operates powerfully as an illusion-producing device that treats as "contradictory" what are in fact separate and autonomous developments, and tries to represent them as 'geneologically' related in a line of dialectical 'descent'. It is, if you like, a kind of anthropomorphism of logic.

The truth, as Gould (for example) has established in his illuminating writings, is that the abiding mark of *historical* development and change is *ad hoc-ness*, not the neat permutations and cancellations of a dialectical logic. What has a history bears traces of its past, and lives in the present through features and capacities "cobbled" together (Gould's word) in an *ad hoc* adaptation and interaction between its contingently given nature and the environments and processes to which it is subject and toward which it is active. (Marx himself inadvertently acknowledges this in the remark encountered earlier in the *Manifesto* where he speaks of "every class handed down from the middle ages".)

To sum up, it is difficult not to conclude that Professor Kaufman's 1872 review of *Capital* in the St. Petersburg *Messenger* reveals him as trading in some (even for that time) unthinking remarks about societies and organisms, tricked out with some handwaving about "science" and "laws", and presented as an account of Marx's "actual method". It is, consequently, even more difficult not to wonder greatly at Marx's being so obviously happy, for the most part, at the reviewer's representation of his "method of inquiry", even to the point of taking the trouble to quote it at length for his readers and posterity.

The only explanation that (in my judgment) renders intelligible this wonder-provoking situation is that Marx is a poor, and often careless, judge of his own work and writings. In particular, when it comes to descriptions of his "method" of explaining social change—whether produced by himself or others—he is not to be relied upon. Part of the argument to this conclusion I have tried to give in this chapter. We have repeatedly seen the ambiguity or confusion of many of Marx's own pronouncements on his theory, and of those of a reviewer to whose account of his work he offers no major dispute. We have also noted the inconsistency of these various pronouncements with many of the things Marx says when he is explaining *actual* social developments or states of affairs. Further argument to this conclusion follows in the next chapter, where we shall examine closely Marx's detailed explanation of the emergence of industrial capitalism in Europe as he presents this in Volume One of *Capital*.

Chapter Four

Marx's Explanation of Historical Change

Do Marx's detailed explanations of actual historical events and fundamental social change constitute a theory of historical change? If they do, what is that theory? In this chapter I seek to answer these questions.

Throughout I shall concentrate on the concluding chapters of the first volume of *Capital,* especially the seven chapters 26 to 32 that comprise Part Eight of the English edition of the book. (In the two German editions, these pages formed one long chapter, numbered 24, which was followed by a final brief chapter 25, numbered 33 in the English edition.) I shall, however, occasionally draw upon earlier passages of *Capital* as well. There are three reasons for choosing to concentrate on these sections from the first volume of *Capital.* The first is that the book itself is a late rather than early work. The second reason is that the book is the most comprehensive and intensely researched piece of writing whose published form Marx himself determined. (The later volumes of *Capital* were prepared for publication by Engels after Marx's death.) The third reason is that the content of these chapters is directly relevant to the question before us. They comprise Marx's fullest discussion of the emergence of capitalism in Western Europe. As such, they are an obvious test case for the claims that Marx has a theory of historical change and that that theory is historical materialism.

I am aware that some persons may wish to object that Marx himself stated, in a letter to the editorial board of the Russian journal *Otechestvennrye Zapiski,* that in these concluding chapters of *Capital I* he is not explaining but describing the emergence of capitalism.[1] My response to this objection is that this disclaimer is exactly what one would expect Marx to say when writing (after the fact) about the relation of these chapters to his putative 'theory'. The truth of Marx's assertion depends on what we find in those chapters. Like any argument from authority, the objection is worthless unless it can survive scrutiny in the manner of any other propositional claim.

1

Marx's project in the pages from *Capital* with which we are concerned is to explain what (following earlier writers) he terms the "primitive accumulation" of capital. In the preceding several hundred pages of his large book, Marx has sought to explain how, in the process of capitalist commodity production, "money is transformed into capital", "surplus-value is made through capital", and "more capital is made from surplus-value" (873). He has also sought to identify many of the social consequences of the capitalist mode of economic life. But this extended analysis of capitalist production has presupposed throughout something not yet addressed: "a primitive accumulation" of capital "which is not the result of the capitalist mode of production but its point of departure" (873). The necessity for such a primitive accumulation proceeds from a fact which Marx has stressed repeatedly up until this point of the book: that capitalism is an historically specific form of economic organization. The point is made here, for example:

> [N]ature does not produce on the one hand owners of money or commodities, and on the other hand men possessing nothing but their own labour power. This relation has no basis in natural history, nor does it have a social basis common to all periods of human history. It is clearly the result of a past historical development, the product of many economic revolutions, of the extinction of a whole series of older formations of social production. (273)

Note the contrast in this passage between 'natural history' and 'human history'. The point of the contrast is to call attention to the social (and so doubly contingent) character of capitalist production. Marx returns to this emphasis early in his discussion of primitive accumulation:

> In themselves, money and commodities are no more capital than the means of production and subsistence are [which last occur in some form in all types of social life]. They need to be transformed into capital. But this transformation can itself only take place under particular circumstances, which meet together at this point: the confrontation of, and the contact between, two very different kinds of commodity owners; on the one hand, the owners of money, means of production, means of subsistence, who are eager to valorize [i.e., increase the value of] the sum of values they have appropriated by buying the labour power of others; on the other hand, free workers, the sellers of their own labour power, . . . [who]

neither form part of the means of production themselves, as would be the case with slaves, serfs, etc., nor do they own means of production, as would be the case with self-employed peasant proprietors . . . With the polarization of the commodity market into these two classes, the fundamental conditions of capitalist production are present. (874)

Note the claim: the *fundamental* conditions of capitalist production are present when there is a *commodity market* of a certain kind. No mention whatever is made of type or development of productive forces. What constitutes the fundamental historical condition for capitalist production is a certain kind of ownership situation: that some persons own only their labour-power, while others own money, means of production and means of subsistence. For a society to have a capitalist mode of production there must, according to Marx, be a certain distribution of that ownership situation: the society must be polarized into large numbers of persons having only their labour-power to sell, and other persons (relatively fewer in number, though they may be many in absolute numbers) who have money, means of production, and means of subsistence, *to whom the rest must sell their labour power in the commodity market*. Capital consists of money, means of production, and means of subsistence, and the "fundamental" condition of capitalism is a society among whose members there is a contrasting relation to capital: some own capital, and the rest lack capital.

Whether this fundamental condition is a sufficient condition for a capitalist mode of production, on Marx's view, I put aside (as an issue to be returned to later). The point is that Marx regards it as a necessary condition, and from its necessity he straightforwardly draws this conclusion:

The process, therefore, which creates the capital-relation can be nothing other than the process which divorces the worker from the ownership of the conditions of his own labour; it is a process which operates [to accomplish] two [historically related] transformations, [1] whereby the social means of subsistence and production are turned into capital, and [2] the immediate producers are turned into wage-labourers. So-called primitive accumulation, therefore, is nothing else than the historical process of divorcing the producer from [ownership of or effective powers over] the means of production. It appears as 'primitive' because it forms the pre-history of capital, and of the mode of production of capital.

Primitive accumulation is not relegated here to 'pre-history' in the sense of 'non-history'. It is described as constituting the pre-history of capitalism. That still places it squarely within human history. In fact, Marx dates the process to a quite recent period in European history:

Marx's Explanation of Historical Change 121

> The economic structure of capitalist society has grown out of the economic structure of feudal society. The dissolution of the latter set free the elements of the former...
> The starting point of the development that gave rise both to the wage labourer and to the capitalist was the enslavement of the worker [under the feudal mode of production]. The advance made [from this initial state] consisted in a change in the form of this servitude, in the transformation of feudal exploitation [of the producer] into capitalist exploitation [of the producer]. To understand the course taken by this change, we do not need to go back very far at all . . . (875)

Marx fixes specifically upon England in tracing the course of this change, and he begins his account with developments in the the fifteenth century on that island.

In explaining his choice of England "as our example", Marx says something that is a reflex nod toward his 'theoretical' agenda. In attending to it, we also touch briefly on an ambiguity in the passage from page 875 just quoted. Marx declares that:

> In the history of primitive accumulation, all revolutions are epoch-making that act as levers for the capitalist class in the course of its formation; but this is true above all for those moments when great masses of men [and women and children] are suddenly and forcibly hurled onto the labour-market as free, unprotected and rightless proletarians. The expropriation of the agricultural producer, of the peasant, from the soil, is the basis of the whole process. (876)

The expropriation of the agricultural producer from the soil *is the basis* — note the words — of the whole process constituting the formation of the capitalist class. Marx then asserts: "The history of this expropriation assumes different aspects in different countries, and runs through its various phases in different orders of succession, and at different times. Only in England, which we therefore take as our example, has it the classic form". (876)

This is a curious remark. How can there be only in England the *classic* form of this process? Against what is the English form of the process adjudged "classic"? The answer of course (running in the teeth of Marx's stress in the sentence before on the great variability of the process in those societies in which it occurs) is some 'theoretical' idea or 'guiding thread' arrived at prior to looking to see how this process actually occurs in specific societies. Mercifully, in the chapters on which we are focusing, this is one of the few moments when we shall find Marx leading his observations and judgments by this 'guiding thread'.

It may be objected that it can hardly turn out that this is what future passages will show, since we have already encountered a remark by Marx quoted a dozen lines back in which he pronounces that "The economic structure of capitalist society has grown out of the economic structure of feudal society." Surely this remark invokes the historical materialist view?

This is an alert objection. But it can be answered. Consider these three sentences:

1. This oak tree has grown out of the acorn that fell.

2. This city has grown out of the scattered villages and towns that were strung along the river bank and valley.

3. This confederation has grown out of the failure of the several independent states to provide an adequate standard of living for their subjects, a failure proceeding from policies of economic protection and trade wars.

The difference between the first of these three assertions and the other two is the difference between organic growth and non-organic growth, which last may be more or less helter-skelter, or systematic, according to conditions and the nature of what is undergoing change. I submit that Marx's sentence should be read on analogy with the second and third type of example, and I point for evidence to what he says immediately after it: "The dissolution of the latter [the economic structure of feudal society] set free the elements of the former" (that is, of the economic structure of capitalist society). This language does not suggest organic growth—the whole of something being transformed into the whole of something else—but something more analogous to the second or third kind of case: some "elements" that had come to exist in the former society were enabled, by its dissolution, to develop ("grow") into something that succeeded it.

If I am right, we require then a story in two stages: why feudal society 'dissolved', and why it was succeeded by capitalism. In fact, Marx runs the two stories together for the most part. This is not altogether unreasonable, since clearly they are connected. The trick is to see, and not lose sight of, how they are connected. In what follows I shall first briefly tease out Marx's account of the dissolution of the economic structure of feudal society, and then trace his explanation of why a capitalist economic structure replaced it. In pursuing this analysis I shall highlight four features of Marx's account: first, the contribution of contingent states of affairs and events; second, the contribution of internal contradictions and tensions within the feudal and capitalist social forms; third, the contribution of force—of effective power exercised by some persons *vis-à-vis* other persons—to the coming about of the respective outcomes; and fourth, the contribution of *unintended consequences* to shaping the course of social change.

2

We may begin by noticing that the third and fourth of these features receive emphasis in the opening pages on primitive accumulation with which we are concerned. Marx declares that

> This primitive accumulation plays approximately the same role in political economy as original sin does in theology. Adam bit the apple, and thereupon sin fell upon the human race . . . Long, long ago [so political economy alleges or presumes] there were two sorts of people: one, the diligent, intelligent and above all frugal elite; the other, lazy rascals, spending their substance, and more, in riotous living. . . Thus it came to pass that the former sort accumulated wealth and the latter sort finally had nothing to sell except their own skins. And from this original sin dates the poverty of the great majority . . . and the wealth of the few that increases constantly . . . In actual history, it is a notorious fact that conquest, enslavement, robbery, murder, in short, *force*, play the greatest part. (873–4, my emphasis)

On the following page, Marx observes that in order for the industrial capitalists ("these new potentates") to achieve the position they now hold in societies structured in accordance with their interests, it was first necessary not only that the "the guild masters of handicrafts, but also the feudal lords" be displaced.

Marx then declares (emphasis mine):

> In this respect, the rise of the industrial capitalists appears as the fruit of a victorious struggle both against feudal power and its disgusting prerogatives, and against the guilds, and the fetters by which the latter restricted the *free development of production* and the free exploitation of man by man. (875)

Note the italicized words, and recall David Landes' emphasis on the important causal role of unrestricted private enterprise in the development of industrial Europe. Marx continues:

> The knights of industry, however, only *succeeded* in supplanting the knights of the sword *by making use of events* [including the actions of others] *in which they had played no part whatsoever.* (875, my emphasis)

Notice Marx's pairing above of "the free development of production and the *free exploitation of man by man*". Capitalist modes of manufacture (and later of industrial production) greatly increased productive capacity. But it does not follow that increasing the productive capacity of "humanity" was the objective of those who sought to escape the "fetters" of the guilds. Their objective was to establish methods of production and fostering social conditions from which *they themselves* could most profit. Thus members of a particular society seeking a freer (because more profitable) "exploitation of man by man" within that society may act in ways that promote "development of production". But what (partly) explains a tendency to development obtaining within this historically particular social situation is a desire by individuals personally to exploit extant market and technological opportunities, not any concern rationally to husband or expand productive capacity on behalf of "humanity".

Here we have an *unintended consequence* of agents' actions entering into the explanation of a social result.

The word "fetters" will have been noted in the above passage—an expression echoing the *Critique* preface and other 'theoretical' pronouncements by Marx. It is used here, however, in an entirely unexceptionable way. I call attention to it because, as we examine Marx's explanation of feudalism's decline and capitalism's rise we shall occasionally encounter similar language evocative of HM. What needs to be remembered is that much of the vocabulary of Marx's theoretical pronouncements is general and flexible enough to be used sensibly in specific contexts, *while still giving Marx* (whenever his choice of language consciously registers) *the impression* that in employing that vocabulary he is keeping faith with its 'theoretically intended' meanings. In such ways may a theorist confuse both himself and his readers.

3

"Our example", to repeat, is England. Throughout his extended account of "the history of primitive accumulation", and especially in his account of "the expropriation of the agricultural producer", Marx focuses on how this development proceeded in one society—England. (Perhaps it would be more correct to say Great Britain, since he occasionally ranges to Scotland and Ireland.) Marx regards that primitive accumulation as connected to the dissolution of the economic structure of feudal society. The connection is twofold. First, the "immediate producer, the worker, could dispose of his own person only after he had ceased to be bound to the soil, and ceased to be the slave or serf of another person" (875). This circumstance was achieved by the (often forcible) appropriation of the land by the "nobility": a process forming a major part of what Marx at one point terms "capitalizing the national means of production and subsistence" (921). Secondly, the accumulation by persons of "usurer's capital and merchant's capital" (914) contributed to the breakdown of the economic structure of feudalism by creating champions and supporters of the centralizing royal power against the "old nobility" (878–9). The dissolution of feudalism is therefore connected to primitive accumulation both as cause and effect. Each of these aspects we must explore in a little detail. In this section we shall investigate why, according to Marx, feudalism did not continue indefinitely. In the next section we shall take up the different but obviously related question: why, according to Marx, was feudalism replaced by "industrial capitalism" rather than some other social form? Throughout both sections, our concern will not be to establish whether Marx's account is true, but to identify what *kind* of explanation he gives of these changes.

Short of extinction of the population by disease or cosmic disaster, there had to be some kind of "social form" in Britain, so long as there were human beings populating the island. Why didn't feudalism continue to be that form? Why was there *basic social change* in England, consisting of feudalism's demise, *and* its replacement by some other social form? Why didn't feudalism continue indefinitely in England?

Marx's answer to this question can be reduced to two claims. The first is that the social and political relations that constituted feudalism produced *self-destructive* conflict that made the English feudal order continually vulnerable to internal or external developments. The second is that external developments did occur that provoked groups in England possessing effective power to pursue projects destructive of the feudal social and political order. These developments external to England were contingent events, which were (in Marx's words) "made use of" by people in England who had "played no part" in causing them. The outcomes of these persons' actions were in turn exploited by groups who were not party to those actions. All of this, notice, is contrary to an HM model of social change as proceeding from the ineluctable development of processes integral to a "social organism".

Both claims by Marx are identifiable in the following frequently quoted passage from Chapter 27 of the English edition. The first few sentences of the passage are not as lucid as one would wish. Nevertheless, the "revolution" they speak of may confidently be identified as what Marx on the following page calls "the revolution in the relations of production". This revolution consisted partly of the nobility's repudiation of feudal land tenure and their effective imposition of a 'private' right property in their estates, and partly of their and the gentry's encroachment on communal land and appropriation of church and state lands. All three developments are identified by Marx as contributing to "divorcing the producer from the means of production" (879)—or, as the French economist Sismondi (quoted by Marx) succinctly expressed it, "separat[ing] every kind of property from every kind of labour" (928).

The prelude of the revolution that laid the foundation of the capitalist mode of production was played out in the last third of the fifteenth century and the first few decades of the sixteenth. A mass of 'free' and unattached proletarians was hurled onto the labour-market by the dissolution of the bands of feudal retainers, who as Sir James Steuart correctly remarked, 'everywhere uselessly filled [great] house and castle' [dynastic strife having been subdued by Henry Tudor]. Although the royal power, itself a product of bourgeois development, forcibly hastened the dissolution of these bands of retainers in its striving for absolute sovereignty, it was by no means the sole cause [note the words] of it. It was rather that the great feudal lords, in their defiant opposition to the king and Parliament, created an incomparably larger proletariat by forcibly driving the peasantry from the land, to which the latter had the same feudal title as the lords themselves, and by usurpation of the common lands. The rapid expansion of wool manufacture in Flanders and the corresponding rise in the price of wool in England provided the direct impulse for these evictions. The old nobility had been devoured by the great feudal wars. The new nobility was the child of its time, for which money was the power of all powers. Transformation of arable land into sheep-walks [for wool production] was therefore its slogan. (878–9)

Several things are distinctive about this passage. One is its reversal of historical materialism's causal sequence. According to HM, what explains social change is change in productive forces. The putative sequence is: first there is revolution in forces of production, causing revolution in social relations to bring them into correspondence with the new forces. Yet in the passage just quoted we see Marx identifying as the "revolution that laid the foundation of the capitalist mode of production" a "revolution in relations of production". As Marx later expresses the matter in his discussion of European colonization in the concluding chapter of the book: "We have seen that the expropriation of the mass of the people from the soil forms the basis of the capitalist mode of production" (934).

What first changed in English feudal society, then, was not forces but relations of production. What provoked that change was an external economic development (rapid expansion of Flemish wool manufacture) which affected the market price, and so the profitabilty in England, of a completely traditional enterprise: wool production. That which immediately accomplished this change in the relations—the "rights or effective powers"—of persons over land was the employment of force; the crudest form of politics. This employment of force is a basic instance of what HM stipulates are "social facts": the exercise of effective power by some persons *vis-à-vis* other persons.

A second distinctive feature of the passage is its appealing to developments in one society to explain developments in another society. A third is its pointing to commercial developments as among the causes of change in relations of production. This last theme is returned to by Marx some pages later in the important chapter "The Genesis of the Industrial Capitalist", where he remarks of the 1860s: "Today, industrial supremacy brings with it commercial supremacy. In the period of manufacture it is the reverse: commercial supremacy produces industrial predominance." (918) We shall return to this and similar statements when considering the rise of industrial capitalism. A fourth feature of the above passage from Chapter 27 is its explicit admission that there may be more than one "sole cause" of important social developments. A fifth is the passage's identifying the pursuit of political hegemony (unaccompanied by any motives or projects for developing productive forces) as among the causes of change in production relations.

All of these explanatory appeals are contrary to HM's representation of how Marx explains social change. So too is the sixth distinctive feature of the passage: its attributing what happened in England partly to the erosion among those persons holding feudal estates of *the attitudes and values* constitutive of feudal social relations, an erosion caused by dynastic wars that arose in great part from those attitudes and relations. In feudal hierarchical relations, "the power of all powers" *was fealty of others to oneself*, receipt of which carried reciprocal obligations of protection and support, but upon which rested one's personal domain over land and those inhabiting it. The greater the domain, the 'greater' the 'lord'. Wealth proceeded primarily from exaction of a surplus from direct producers 'bound' to one as serfs, and power derived most directly from the command and maintenance of bodies of armed men. In such a social order, increase of wealth and power was mainly to be got by dispossessing others. The consequence was a constant tendency of such a social structure to generate dynastic strife and warfare. In England, in the fifteenth century especially, a high proportion of lords and sons of lords perished in the wars between 'Lancaster' and 'York' over possession of the English throne, with its prize of the greatest 'domain' of all, the 'king-dom[ain]'. When heads or heirs of noble houses were killed in these bloodlettings, *someone had to succeed to their place and role*. Increasingly, promotion of new entrants to the nobility was made (through marriage or outright appointment) from among the wealthy burgesses of the towns.

These were people who had made their wealth and had their values and attitudes shaped by commercial activity. They naturally favoured a centralizing royal power against an unruly and "defiant" nobility. They also regarded money as "the power of all powers". Hence when a greatly profitable commercial opportunity arose for which "sheep-walks" were needed, these persons saw no obstacle to evicting the peasants forcibly from the land. These persons among the ruling families of England did not oppose change in social relations and practice, but sought to exploit the new market opportunities. For them fealty came a poor second to coin of the realm.

In short, according to Marx, a basic cause of that expropriation of the agricultural producer from the soil that "forms the basis of the capitalist mode of production" is change in the attitudes and values of those persons commanding effective power over means of production. This change is itself importantly explained by the self-destructive dynamic of feudal social relations. This self-destructive dynamic made frequent change in the ruling personnel of feudal England greatly probable. It therefore made eventual erosion of feudal attitudes and relationships greatly probable. Hence an important part of the explanation of the eventual dissolution of feudal society in England is this self-destructive dynamic. Another part of the explanation is the fact of royal ambitions to establish absolute sovereignty; another is the existence of towns based on commercial activity from among whose wealthiest citizens appointments to noble estate are made; and a further part of the explanation is the fact of commercial opportunities in wool created by economic developments outside England.

One might express the matter most simply by stating that, in Marx's analysis, the nature of feudal relations of production and appropriation made feudal society prone to change, and events transpired over time which caused that to which feudalism was vulnerable to come about. Both the character of the feudal social form, and facts not constitutive of feudalism, contribute to causing the outcome. In the early and decisive stages of this process, none of the causal factors *integral to England* involve development of productive forces or growth of human productive capacity (whichever idiom is preferred).

It may be objected by some readers that productive forces do figure in Marx's analysis, in two ways. The rapid expansion of wool manufacture in Flanders may be alleged to be a case of growth of human productive capacity, as may the embarking upon (and achievement of) increased wool production in England. The objection does not stand up, however. To take the second of these features first, increased wool production was neither pursued as growth of overall productive capacity in England, nor did it constitute *of itself growth of overall* productive capacity of the society. One immediate effect of enclosure for sheep-walks was the relative impoverishment of large numbers of persons (as contemporary observers quoted by Marx report). This impoverishment proceeded from the shift of resource use from subsistence agriculture directly satisfying domestic human needs to commodity production satisfying (to a substantial degree) market demands *external* to the producing society. Profits from such production, where they were not recapitalized, went to funding the abundant consumption of a few. It is true that the enclosure of arable lands for sheep-walks probably contributed in the long term to more efficient and/or intensive farming practices in England, yielding greater per unit outputs in crops and animal husbandry. But that was an unintended, and, in great part, much later result, not an operative cause. In Chapter 30 entitled "The Impact" (note the word) " of the Agricultural Revolution on Industry", Marx opens his discussion with these remarks (emphases are mine):

> The intermittent but constantly renewed expropriation and expulsion of the agricultural population [extending from the late fifteenth to the eighteenth century] supplied the urban industries . . . with a mass of proletarians standing entirely outside the corporate guilds and unfettered by them . . . The thinning out of the [remaining] self-supporting peasants corresponded directly with the concentration of the industrial proletariat . . . But this was not the *only consequence* [of that expropriation]. In spite of the smaller number of its cultivators, the soil brought forth as much as before, and even more, because the revolution in property relations on the land was *accompanied* [not, notice, caused] by improved methods of cultivation, greater co-operation [Marx means especially greater division of labour], a higher concentration of the means of production [into much larger productive units, through enclosures] and so on, and because the agricultural wage-labourers were made to work at a higher level of intensity, and the field of production on which they [as a class of producers] worked for themselves shrank more and more. (908)

Turning to the Flemish wool manufacture, let us suppose (for the sake of argument) that this Flemish manufacture constituted increased productive capacity and output in Flanders (an increase proceeding, however, not from new technology but from recruitment of rural producers and from cost-efficiencies introduced by entrepreneurial mercantile organization). This economic development on the continent created a market for English wool production that drove up the price (and so the profitability) of English wool sold either domestically or in the export wool trade. Still, this development is not of the kind historical materialism posits, since (as has already been stressed) these developments are not an instance of growth of productive capacity in England, provoking basic social change aimed at removing internal "fetters" on the continuation and expansion of that growth. It is (we are allowing for argument's sake) growth of productive capacity in a *different society*, provoking change in production relations in England.

Furthermore, these changes are instituted (in Marx's "example") not by subordinate groups whose interests lie with advancement of new productive forces, *but by persons already exercising economic and political hegemony* whose economic interests are contingently advanced in present market conditions by replacement of one traditional use of means of production in land by another traditional use. The picture is not HM's scenario of basic social change being caused by change in productive forces, and accomplished by persons whose interests these new forces serve, and who displace, through political struggle, the previous ruling group. In Marx's example of England, it is the extant ruling group, altered in composition and attitude by developments proceeding from its own systemic relations, who institute the changes that are said by Marx to comprise "the basis of the capitalist mode of production".

In relating briefly Marx's account of the dissolution of feudalism, I have purposely concentrated on only some of the factors he invokes in explanation. However, one factor thus far ignored should be briefly noted, since we discussed it in the first chapter. Marx at one point declares that "The process of forcible expropriation of the people received a new and terrible impulse in the sixteenth century from the Reformation, and the consequent [note the word] colossal spoliation of church property" (881). This property was vast, since the church was "the feudal proprietor of a great part of the soil of England" (881). In treating of these developments Marx calls specific attention to the resulting evictions of tenants from church lands, and to the loss by the poor of their legal right to relief out of church tithes and of the benefits of monastic charity. He then remarks:

> These immediate results of the Reformation were not its *most lasting* ones. The property of the church formed the religious bulwark of the old conditions of landed property. With its fall, these conditions could no longer maintain their existence. (882–3, my emphasis)

Notice that what is said to be the most lasting result of the Reformation, because *one cause* of the dissolution of the old conditions of landed property, is the removal of the political and *normative* obstacle that unreformed Catholicism, and extensive church property, presented to any repudiation of feudal rights and tenure in land. Marx connects the Reformation and the capitalization of the nation's soil, but he does not identify capitalization as causing the Reformation. Rather, he cites the Reformation as giving that capitalization of the nation's soil which is already under way "a new and terrible impulse". At the same time, the causal importance assigned here by Marx to normative beliefs and commitments is obvious.

One might recapitulate Marx's account of the feudal nobility's "abolish[ing of] the feudal tenure in land" with an assertion by the Scottish economist David Buchanan in 1814 which Marx himself quotes in a footnote: "The land, formerly . . . was peopled in proportion to its produce, but under the new system . . . the population [working the land] is reduced, not to what the land will maintain, but to what it will [profitably] employ" (891). Among Marx's own several summations is this one:

The spoilation of the Church's property [under the Tudors], the fraudulent alienation of the state domains [following the 1660 Restoration], the theft of the common lands, the usurpation of feudal and [in Scotland] clan property under circumstances of ruthless terrorism, all these things were just so many idyllic methods of primitive accumulation. They conquered the field for capitalist agriculture, incorporated the soil into capital, and created for the urban industries the necessary supplies of free and rightless proletarians. (895)

It is to "urban industry" that we must now turn.

4

Early in his discussion of primitive accumulation Marx declares that though "the first sporadic traces of capitalist production" occur "as early as the fourteenth or fifteenth centuries in certain towns of the Mediterranean, the capitalist era dates from the sixteenth century" (876). In his account of the emergence of that era, he concentrates on three developments. The first we have already considered: "the expropriation and partial eviction of the rural population" from the land (915). The second development, closely related to the first, Marx terms the "genesis of the capitalist farmer" (905). The third development he terms the "genesis of the industrial capitalist" (914). As with his account of the expropriation of the rural population, Marx's treatment of these latter two developments is not very clearly set out. But the *kind* of explanation given is wholly evident.

According to Marx, "the only class created directly by the expropriation of the agricultural population is the great landed proprietors". In contrast, "the genesis of the farmers . . . is a slow process evolving through many centuries", and beginning in England as early as "the second half of the fourteenth century" (905). In other words, the emergence of the capitalist farmer is a process independent of, but complementary to (and increasingly hastened by), the expropriation of the bulk of the agricultural population by the feudal magnates. The first farmers, in Marx's account, were originally serfs who held appointment as bailiffs on the lord's estate. In time these persons became share-croppers, at first using "seed, cattle and farm implements" provided by the 'land'-'lord' (note the derivation of the word), but in time more and more employing their own capital outlay. From the beginning these persons are distinguished by the fact that each "exploits more wage labour than the other tenanted peasants". The eventual outcome—achieved "quickly in England"—is "the farmer properly so-called, who valorizes his own capital by employing wage-labourers, and pays a part of the surplus product, in money or in kind, to the landlord as ground rent" (905). Then comes the intersection of this development with that already considered above:

> During the fifteenth century the independent peasant [who is not a serf but a tenant holding a long lease], and the farm-labourer working for himself [on his own small property] as well as for wages, enriched themselves by their own labour; and as long as this was the case, both the farmer's circumstance and his field of production remained mediocre. But the agricultural revolution [in social relations regarding land] which began in the last third of the fifteenth century, and continued during the bulk of the sixteenth (excepting, however, its last few decades), enriched him just as quickly as it impoverished the mass of the agricultural folk. (906)

Marx points to three things from which this enrichment proceeded. Two of these he reports immediately, and the other he relegates to the following section of the book. This last of the three is the most general, and consists in the fact that the expropriation of agricultural lands formerly under feudal tenure, and the enclosure of land formerly open to common use, created a domestic commodity market in agricultural products serviceable by those persons who still had production rights over arable land or pasture. This fact is directly connected to one of the factors Marx immediately mentions: "The usurpation of the common lands allowed the farmer to augment greatly his stock of cattle [through purchases from those now lacking access to pasture], almost without cost, while the cattle themselves yielded a richer supply of manure for the cultivation of the soil" (906). The third factor, described by Marx as "of decisive importance", was the "progressive fall in the value of precious metals" caused by the entry into Europe from the Americas of large quantities of gold and silver during the sixteenth century, which windfall development "brought golden fruit to the farmers" in two forms. This deflation of money, combined with the surplus of expropriated agricultural labourers, "lowered [real] wages", with the consequence that a "portion of the latter was now added to the profits of the farmer" (906). At the same time, while the "continuous rise [both from inflation and demand] in the [real] prices of corn, wool, meat, in short of all agricultural products, swelled the money capital of the farmer without any action on his part", leading to the result that "the ground rent he had to pay diminished, since it had been contracted for on the basis of the old money values" (906).

The upshot is that "England, at the end of the sixteenth century, had a class of [nonnoble] capitalist farmers who were rich men in relation to the circumstances of the time" (907). This outcome, notice, is explained as proceeding from several causes, some fortuitous and external to England, some consisting of changes in the social relations of production, and most of them instances of persons "making use of [contingent] developments in which they had played no part" (875).

Marx, we have seen, relates the rise of "the capitalist farmer" both to "the agricultural revolution" in property relations in land and to the development of improved methods of agricultural production. (See the passage quoted above at page 219.) But he also connects it to the rise of industrial capitalism—to production by means of machines, not by "manufacture" using traditional implements such as hand-looms and spinning wheels. The connection is one of mutually supporting interest. To state it most briefly, both capitalist agriculture and capitalist industry favour a situation in which all persons must acquire the means of subsistence necessary to human life and satisfaction *on the commodity market*. Hence capitalist farmers encouraged the replacement of traditional manufacturing by the industrial mode of production, because such a development reduced the number of persons who could subsist on the produce of small plots of land supplemented by wages got from the putting out system of manufacture. Meanwhile, the "mill towns" increased the extent and stability of the capitalist agricultural market by increasing the numbers of those who had both the need and sufficient money income to resort to the agricultural produce market. At the same time, machine production increased the demand by industry (arising from greatly increased outputs) for wool, skins, grain, food stuffs, and so on. As Marx expresses it:

> [O]nly the destruction of rural domestic industry can give the home market of a country [both agricultural and non-agricultural] that extension and stability which the capitalist mode of production [which is production for profitable sale, not subsistence, optimally] requires.... [T]he manufacturing period, properly so called, does not succeed in carrying out this transformation radically and completely.... A consistent foundation for capitalist agriculture could only be provided by large-scale industry in the form of machinery; it is large-scale industry which radically [that is, physically and irretrievably] expropriates the vast majority of the agricultural population and completes the divorce between agriculture and rural domestic industry, tearing up the latter's roots, which are spinning and weaving. It therefore also conquers the entire home market for industrial capital, for the first time. (913)

The next question we must take up is: from whence comes the"the industrial capitalist" engaged in "large-scale industry"?

5

Marx begins his answer to this question with the pronouncement: "The genesis of the industrial capitalist did not proceed in such a gradual way as that of the farmer" (914). Yet this remark is to some extent at odds with the pages that follow it. Marx ordinarily means by the expression 'industrial capitalist' someone whose capital is directed toward production by means of machinery. Thus the industrial capitalist only appears in the late eighteenth century. Furthermore, Marx tends to equate "the capitalist mode of production" with capitalist-financed large-scale machine production. Nevertheless, the "genesis" of industrial capitalism, as Marx relates it, is a relatively gradual process, if not so gradual as that of capitalist agriculture. Both the mode of social relations that comprises capitalist commodity production (of which industrial capitalism is an instance) and the capital accumulations that eventually were devoted to industrial production (either directly or as loan financing) emerged in Europe in the "medieval" period. These were adapted, expanded and duplicated, in response to developing events and opportunities, until the form of economic organization of several European societies was predominantly or wholly "capitalist". Marx expressly states:

> Doubtless many small guild-masters, and a still greater number of independent small artisans, or even wage-labourers, transformed themselves into small capitalists, and, by gradually extending their exploitation of wage-labour and the corresponding accumulation, into 'capitalists' without qualification [by which I take Marx to mean capitalists who play no direct part in the physical labour of production]. In the period when capitalist production was in its infancy things often happened as they had done in the period of infancy of the medieval town, where the question as to which escaped serfs should be master and which servant was in great part decided by the earlier or later date of their flight. (914)

The "infancy" of capitalist production is surely part of the "genesis" of industrial capitalism. Noteworthy here is Marx's linking this beginning to the perennial pursuit by individuals of increased means of satisfying their wants, leading some to attempt to escape existing restraints upon that pursuit and to exploit whatever economic opportunities they discern in their society. For the developments in question these opportunities especially involved market transactions, as Marx goes on to state (my emphasis):

> The snail's pace of advance [of small-scale capitalist exploitation of market opportunities] under this [*ad hoc*] method by no means corresponded with the commercial requirements of the new world market, which had been created by the great discoveries of the end of the fifteenth century. But the Middle Ages had handed down two distinct forms of capital, *which ripened in the most varied economic formations* of society, and which, before the era of the capitalist mode of production, nevertheless functioned as capital—usurer's capital and merchant's capital. (914)

Note again the stress on the decisive causal role played by market developments provoking commercial pursuits. Note too the express reference to capital and capitalist activities emerging in a variety of types of economic structure.

Marx then declares (in remarks recalling those concerning agriculture) that the "money capital formed by means of usury and commerce was prevented from turning into industrial capital by the feudal organization of the countryside and the guild organization of the towns" (915). However, these "fetters vanished with the dissolution of the feudal bands of retainers, and the expropriation and partial eviction of the rural population" (915). We see Marx here anachronistically imposing on the period in question a preoccupation got from hindsight. Surely what, at the time in question, most prevented capital got by usury and commerce from turning into industrial capital was the fact that the kinds of machine necessary for this had not yet been invented. Nor were they invented until the greatly profitable manufacturing production based on traditional technologies (but more and more exploiting the concentration of producers in factories, the specialization of tasks, and the exacting of a much longer working day) created a market for such output-enhancing machines. What Marx can only sensibly mean here is that the employment of capital in the ways that led to industrial capitalism was not possible so long as the feudal organization of the countryside and towns was intact. The changes constituting "the revolution in relations of production" (879) that began with the expropriation of many of the agricultural population enabled circumvention of these "fetters" by establishing "manufactures . . . at sea ports, and at points in the countryside which were beyond the control of the municipalities and their guilds" (915). An immediate consequence in England was "the bitter struggle of the corporate towns [i.e., those with charters of incorporation and traditional guild organizations] against these new seed-beds of industry" (915).

However, the capital "handed down" from the Middle Ages does not, in Marx's account, represent the most decisive source of the primitive accumulation that directly precipitated that development of capitalist manufacturing production which eventually grew into industrial capitalism. Rather (recalling developments already touched upon):

> The discovery of gold and silver in America, the extirpation, enslavement and entombment in mines of the indigenous population of that continent, the beginnings of the conquest and plunder of India, and the conversion of Africa into a preserve for the commercial hunting of blackskins, are . . . the chief moments of primitive accumulation. Hard on their heels follows the commercial war of the European nations, which has the globe as its battlefield. It begins with the revolt of the Netherlands from Spain, assumes gigantic dimensions in England's Anti-Jacobin [i.e., anti-French] War, and is still going on in the shape of the Opium Wars against China, etc. (915)

Marx follows his reference to England in this passage with a further comment involving England which makes clear that his talk of "moments" in these sentences (an idiom evocative of Hegel) in fact refers to methods. In this further comment he also reiterates his emphasis that the accumulation of the capital upon which industrial capitalism is founded is a truly 'primitive' accumulation in that it proceeds from a forcible seizure or forced production of wealth (or the means of producing wealth):

> The different moments of primitive accumulation can be assigned in particular to Spain, Portugal, Holland, France and England, in more or less chronological order. These different moments are systematically combined together at the end of the seventeenth century in England: the combination embraces the colonies, the national debt, the modern tax system, and the [tariff] system of protection. These methods [note the word] depend in part on brute force, for instance the colonial system. But they all employ the power of the state, the concentrated and organized force of society, to hasten, as in a hothouse, the process of transformation of the feudal mode of production into the capitalist mode, and to shorten the transition. Force is the midwife of every old society which is pregnant with a new one. It is itself an economic power. (915–6)

In this famous passage we see a return of the organic analogy discussed in the previous chapter. Marx, in a pair of mixed metaphors, speaks first of state power hastening as in a hothouse the transformation of feudalism into capitalism. He then refers to state power as the midwife of every old society pregnant with a new one. These metaphors are, for the reasons given earlier, inappropriate as representations of the development in question, and are one more instance of the kind of careless and backward-looking characterization trading on hindsight that prompts the "historical materialist" construction of Marx's writings. What is important in the passage is its explicit description of coercion as "an economic power". Coercive force, in other words, is one cause of economic change. But coercive force is a paradigm of what HM terms social facts: the exercise of effective power by some persons over other persons. Indeed Marx himself explicitly speaks of the contribution state power makes, by the several devices listed, to the development of capitalism as an exercise of "the concentrated and organized force of society".

6

Up to this point we have been attending to Marx's account of feudalism's collapse and capitalism's emergence. We have seen that an important part of

Marx's Explanation of Historical Change

Marx's explanation of why feudalism declined involves appeal to an internal self-destructive dynamic of the feudal social order. A similar situation obtains when we turn to Marx's explanation of the alleged future collapse of capitalism and its replacement by socialism. Here too Marx stresses an internal incoherence of the system. Capitalist relations, Marx claims, have a self-destructive logic which must inescapably cause their eventual demise.

The most famous statement by Marx of this prognostication occurs in the *Communist Manifesto*, which asserts two complementary developments in capitalism. The first is the progressive immiseration of productive labour.

> Hitherto, every form of society has been based . . . on the antagonism of oppressing and oppressed classes. But in order to oppress a class, certain conditions must be assured to it under which it can, at least, continue its slavish existence. . . . The modern labourer [under capitalism] . . . instead of rising with the progress of industry, sinks deeper and deeper below the conditions of existence of his own class. He becomes a pauper, and pauperism develops more rapidly than population and wealth. And here it becomes evident, that the bourgeoisie is unfit any longer to be the ruling class in society, and to impose [note the word] its conditions of existence upon society as an over-riding law . . . because it is incompetent to assure an existence to its slave within his slavery . . .[2]

The second and parallel development is the progressive politicization and organization of the working class.

> The essential condition for the existence, and for the sway of the bourgeois class, is the formation and augmentation of capital; the condition for capital is wage-labour. Wage-labour rests exclusively on competition between the labourers. [I take this statement to assert that the price paid wage-labour is determined exclusively by competition; one of many assertions by Marx which contradict the labour theory of value.] The advance of industry, whose involuntary promoter [note the adjective] is the bourgeoisie, replaces the isolation of the labourers, due to competition, by their revolutionary combination, due to association. The development of Modern Industry, therefore, cuts from under its feet the very foundation on which the bourgeoisie produces and appropriates products. What the bourgeoisie, therefore, produces, above all, is its own grave-diggers. Its fall and the victory of the proletariat are equally inevitable.[3]

The truth or falsehood of these allegations is not our concern here. The issue for us is the kind of explanation being given by Marx, which can readily be seen to have no necessary connection to HM's Development or Primacy Theses. To take just one aspect of the matter: that every capitalist wishes his own employees to be satisfied with subsistence wages, but wishes the employees of all other capitalists to have disposable income enabling them to buy his products, generates a contradictory dynamic in capitalism whose consequences hold irrespective of HM's theses about productive development.

Capitalism, according to Marx, develops the productive capacity to meet adequately human needs, but embeds that capacity in a social structure subordinating it to the pursuit of profit. At the same time, capitalism develops a labouring class so placed as eventually to develop the knowledge, will, and collective power enabling it to replace that social structure with one answering human needs. This is the position taken by Marx as early as 1848. It is also the position continued in *Capital I*.

In the long and important Chapter 15 on "Machinery and Large-Scale Industry" (comprising roughly 150 pages of the book) we find Marx excoriating "our economic apologists" for capitalism in these terms:

> The contradictions and antagonisms inseparable from the capitalist application of machinery do not exist, they say, because they [these contradictions and antagonisms] do not arise out of machinery as such, but out of its capitalist application! Therefore, since machinery in itself shortens the hours of labour, but when employed by capital it lengthens them; since in itself it lightens labour, but when employed by capital it heightens its intensity; since in itself it is a victory of man over the forces of nature but in the hands of capital it makes man the slave of those forces; since in itself it increases the wealth of the producers, but in the hands of capital it makes them into paupers, the bourgeois economist simply states that the contemplation of machinery in itself demonstrates with exactitude that all these evident contradictions are a mere semblance, present in everyday reality, but not existing in themselves, and therefore having no theoretical existence either. (568–9)

Forty pages later Marx spells out more fully the contradictions inherent in the capitalist form of large-scale social production.

> Modern industry never views or treats the existing form of a production process as the definitive one. Its technical basis is therefore revolutionary, whereas [the technical bases of] all earlier modes of production were essentially conservative. By means of machinery, chemical processes and other methods, it is continually transforming not only the technical basis of production but also the functions of the worker and the social combinations of the labour process. At the same time, it thereby also revolutionizes the division of labour within society, and incessantly throws masses of capital and of workers from one branch of production to another. (617)

Marx then goes on to repeat that among the consequences of the "absolute contradiction" between the "revolutionary" character of the technical basis of capitalism and the "brutal" (621) and unyielding social form within which this innovating technology is exploited are the doing away with "all fixity and all security so far as the worker's life-situation is concerned", "the ceaseless human sacrifices required from the working class, . . . the reckless squandering of labour-powers, and . . . the devastating effects of social anarchy" (618). A few pages later he calls attention to the unintended effects of public efforts to regulate conditions of work:

> If the general extension of factory legislation to all trades for the purpose of protecting the working class in mind and body has become [note the tense] inevitable, on the other hand, as we have already pointed out, that extension hastens on the general conversion of numerous isolated small industries into a few combined industries carried on upon a large scale; it therefore accelerates the concentration of capital and the exclusive predominance of the factory system. It destroys both the 'ancient' and transitional forms behind which the dominion of capital is still partially hidden, and replaces them with a dominion which is direct and unconcealed. But by doing this it also generalizes the direct struggle against its rule. . . . [T]he result of the immense impetus given to technical improvement by the limitation and regulation of the working day is to increase the anarchy and the proneness to catastrophe of capitalist production as a whole, the intensity of labour, and the competition of machinery with the worker. (635)

It is worth noting that two sentences later Marx asserts that these developments, by "maturing" the " contradictions and antagonisms of the capitalist form" of large-scale machine production, work to "ripen " (Marx's word) "*both* the elements for forming a new society *and* the forces tending towards the overthrow of the old one" (635, my emphasis). Here we have the language of organic growth side by side with language sensitive to the difference between two distinguishable processes: dissolution of the old social form, and emergence of a new social form.

We find, then, in *Capital*, as in the earlier *Manifesto*, an explanation of the alleged future demise of capitalism which is continuous in one respect with Marx's explanation of the demise of feudalism. In each case, an important part of the explanation is the alleged existence of an internal dynamic which generates incoherences and antagonisms destructive of the existing social form.

Furthermore, in *Capital I* we find Marx explicitly assigning an important causal role to two further sets of inescapably social facts: the centralization of capital, and the credit system. We also discover Marx attributing (with notable prescience, and in direct tension with other aspects of his thought) the inviability of capitalism partly to environmental degradation. I wish to look briefly at these issues before concluding.

7

We have already paid close attention to Marx's emphasis on "a certain accumulation of capital in the hands of individual producers" as being "the historical basis, instead of the historical result, of specifically capitalist production" (775). Marx repeatedly stresses that "the development of the social productivity of labour presupposes co-operation on a large scale" (775). At the same time, he continually affirms that co-operation on a large scale "can be realized only through an increase of individual capitals, only in proportion as the social means of production and subsistence are transformed into the private property of capitalists" (775). Thus (once more) social relations of a certain kind are held by Marx to be a basic cause of the historical developments by which "the production process can be transformed into a process of the technological application of scientific knowledge" (775)

In the long Chapter 25 that precedes those on primitive accumulation (and from which chapter the above quotations are taken), Marx discusses at one point what he calls the "centralization of capitals" (777). This consists in "a change in the distribution of already available and already functioning capital" (777). This change does not entail any increase in the quantity of capital available to the society. The change is a change in ownership and control, not in magnitude. (The phenomenon is the now familiar one of 'acquisitions and mergers'.) Alongside the growing centralization of capital there arises, Marx declares, "an altogether new force" which "comes into existence with the development of capitalist production: the credit system" (777).

This credit system is described by Marx as "the specific machine for the centralization of capitals". "In its turn", Marx asserts, "centralization becomes one of the greatest levers" of the development and extension of "the specifically capitalist mode of production" (778n).

> It shortens and quickens the transformation of separate processes of production into processes socially combined and carried out on a large scale. The increasing bulk of individual masses of capital become the material basis [note the words] of an uninterrupted revolution in the mode of production itself. The capitalist mode of [large scale machine] production continually conquers branches of industry not yet wholly, or only sporadically or formally, subjugated to it. (778n)

Here we see Marx identifying as the material basis of those changes in the technical mode of production that constitute industrial capitalism, a change in the distribution of ownership of capital—another paradigmatically social fact. Should anyone think that the words 'material basis' do not imply any causal contribution here, but denote a mere background condition, the sentences that directly follow rebut this thought.

At first, it is the mere adding of new capital to old which allows the objective conditions of the process of production to be extended and undergo technical transformations. But soon these changes of composition, and technical transformations, get a more or less complete grip on all the old [especially fixed] capital that has reached the term of its period of reproduction [i.e., of profitable deployment] and therefore has to be replaced [i.e., reconstituted or re-deployed]. This metamorphosis of old capital is independent, to a certain extent, of the absolute growth of social capital, in the same way as is its centralization. But this centralization, which only redistributes the social capital already to hand, and melts a number of old capitals into one, works in its turn as *a powerful agent* in the metamorphosis of old capital. (778n, my emphasis)

A further parameter of the self-destructive dynamic attributed by Marx to capitalism parallels that already noted in which "the increase in the productivity and the mobility of labour is purchased at the cost of laying waste and debilitating labour-power itself" (638). This further aspect of the dynamic concerns the relation of capitalist production to the ecology of human living. Capitalist industry leads to the concentration of the population in large urban centers, which "disturbs the metabolic interaction between man and the earth, i.e., it prevents the return to the soil of its constituent elements consumed by man in the form of food and clothing" (637). Marx then goes on to observe:

Moreover, all progress in capitalist agriculture is a progress in the art, not only of robbing the worker, but of robbing the soil; all progress in increasing the fertility of the soil for a given time is a progress towards ruining the more long-lasting sources of that fertility. The more a country proceeds from largescale industry as the background of its development, as in the case of the United States, the more rapid is this process of destruction. Capitalist production, therefore, only develops the techniques and the degree of combination of the social process of production by simultaneously undermining the original sources of all wealth—the soil and the worker. (638)

8

In examining Marx's explanation of the demise of feudalism in England and its replacement by industrial capitalism as this is presented in the concluding chapters of *Capital I*, we have found Marx's reasoning to contrast sharply with that required by historical materialism. Had Marx placed these concluding chapters at, or near, the beginning of his book, where they most appropriately belong, it is probable that we would have heard much less of 'Marxism' and 'historical materialism' than has been the case. Reinforcing the early sections of *The Communist Manifesto* (which we have seen they parallel), these chapters should have given pause to readers inclined to build upon the *dicta* of the 1859 preface and other passages from Marx's writings. That the historical materialist construction of Marx's writings has won virtual unanimity as the accepted reading of his account of social change is an object lesson in the consequences of crediting a writer's pronouncements over his or her practice.

We have also found Marx's explanation of the predicted decline of capitalism and triumph of socialism to rest on arguments unconnected to HM's representation of his thought. The outcome is to open the question whether Marx's writings have more to offer students of society than their widespread description as 'Marxist' has led people to believe. To this question I now briefly turn.

However, before doing so I wish to conclude this chapter by quoting three sentences from the very early *German Ideology*, written by Marx and Engels in 1845–6 but not published until 1932. The sentences are an apt epitaph to the preceding four chapters, and evidence that even some of the pronouncements of Marx align with his practice.

> History is nothing but the succession of the separate generations, each of which exploits the materials, the capital funds, the productive forces handed down to it by all the preceding generations, and thus, on the one hand, continues the traditional activity in completely changed circumstances and, on the other, modifies the old circumstances with a completely changed activity. This can be speculatively distorted so that later history is made the goal of earlier history, e.g., the goal ascribed to the discovery of America is to further the eruption of the French Revolution. Thereby history receives its own special aims and becomes 'a person ranking with other persons' (to wit: 'Self Consciousness, Criticism, the Unique', etc.), while what is designated with the words 'destiny', 'goal', 'germ', or 'ideal' of earlier history is nothing more than an abstraction formed from later history, from the active influence which earlier history exercises on later history.[4]

Chapter Five

Reading Marx

My intention in this brief concluding chapter is to produce some reasons why Marx's writings should claim the attention of anyone who seeks to understand and appraise the contemporary human condition. In arguing this I shall touch upon a range of issues which constitute abiding, if not always explicitly announced, preoccupations of Marx throughout his writings. In touching upon them, I shall also identify some further errors and blind alleys that Marx's writings—and their engagement by others—should counsel us to avoid.

Marx, I have argued, has suffered from a failure by readers to distinguish carefully the theorist from the theory. In this fate he is himself implicated, as we have seen. Yet there is an irony attending Marx's reception at the hands of readers which bears attention. The irony is that while readers of Marx's pages on historical change have been too willing to control their reading by Marx's pronouncements about what he has established and holds, in relation to other issues they have sometimes not attended closely enough to Marx's theoretical and methodological directions. While too ready to credit Marx's self-descriptions in the one case, readers have ignored Marx's theoretical discriminations in others.

An apt example is Marx's statements about justice in *Capital I*, about which a lively controversy has raged in the last few decades involving Allen Wood, Richard Miller, and others.[1] The controversy concerns whether or not Marx repudiated moral distinctions and moral reasoning. Two passages in *Capital I* that have figured extensively in this controversy are these, from sections 1 and 2 of Chapter 7.

> Suppose that a capitalist pays for a day's worth of labour-power; then the right to use that power for a day belongs to him, just as much as the right to use any other commodity, such as a horse he had hired for the day. The use of a commodity

belongs to its purchaser, and the seller of the labour-power, by giving his labour, does no more, in reality, than part with the use-value that he has sold. From the instant he steps into the workshop, the use-value of his labour-power and therefore also its use, which is labour, belongs to the capitalist. By the purchase of labour-power, the capitalist incorporates labour, as a living agent of fermentation, into the lifeless constituents of the product, which also belong to him. . . . The labour process is a process between things the capitalist has purchased, things which belong to him. Thus the product of this process belongs to him just as much as the wine which is the product of the process of fermentation going on in his cellar. (292)

The owner of money has paid the value of a day's labour-power; he therefore has the use of it for a day, a day's labour belongs to him. On the one hand the daily sustenance of labour-power costs [let us suppose] only half a day's labour, while on the other hand the very same labour-power can remain effective, can work, during a whole day, and consequently the value which its use during one day creates is double what the capitalist pays for that use; this circumstance is a piece of good luck for the buyer, but by no means an injustice towards the seller. (301)

These sentences have been held by many readers of *Capital* to establish that Marx repudiates the view that exchanges between capitalists and workers are unjust exchanges. The passages are alleged to be among many in which Marx can be seen to reject morality as a 'pre-socialist' phenomenon.

The sentences are from the seventh chapter of *Capital I*, entitled "The Labour Process and the Valorization Process". But this chapter can only be read correctly against the background of the chapter preceding it, entitled "The Sale and Purchase of Labour Power". In that sixth chapter Marx says such extremely relevant things as the following. (All emphases are mine.)

[I]n order that the owner of money may find labour-power on the market as a commodity, various conditions must first be fulfilled. *In and for itself*, the exchange of commodities implies no other relations of dependence than those which result from its own nature. *On this assumption*, labour-power can appear on the market as a commodity only if, and in so far as, its possessor, the individual whose labour-power it is, offers it for sale or sells it as a commodity. In order that its possessor may sell it as a commodity, he must have it at his disposal, he must be the free proprietor of his own labour-power, hence of his person. He and the owner of money meet in the market, and enter into relations with each other on a footing of equality *as owners of commodities*, with the sole difference that one is a buyer, the other a seller; both are therefore equal *in the eyes of the law*. (270–1)

The second essential condition which allows the owner of money to find labour-power in the market as a commodity is this, that the possessor of labour-power, instead of being able to sell commodities in which his labour has been objectified, must rather be compelled to offer for sale as a commodity that very labour-power which exists only in his living body. (272)

Why this free worker confronts him in the sphere of circulation is a question which does not interest the owner of money, for he finds the labour-market in existence as a particular branch of the commodity-market. *And for the present* it interest us just as little. We confine ourselves to the fact *theoretically*, as he does practically. (273)

This perspective is expressly continued in Chapter Seven. Indeed, it is observable in the very sentences from that chapter under consideration. If the reader will look back to the remarks quoted above from page 292, he or she will note Marx's statement that *"from his"* — the capitalist's — "point of view, the labour process is nothing more than the consumption of the commodity purchased", and so on.

In short, in the sentences in question Marx can only be interpreted as repudiating considerations of justice if readers ignore Marx's own express directives as to how his engagement with these market transactions is to be understood.

This, of course, is not the only kind of mistake underlying the widespread view that Marx repudiated morality as a 'bourgeois' phenomenon. Another is the error of thinking that it is necessary to use such words as 'moral', 'right', or 'wrong' to be judging morally. The truth is that to judge morally is to judge by appeal to what are *moral considerations*,[2] and this we find Marx doing again and again throughout his writings, and not only appealing to them but appealing passionately to the reader (often in explicitly moral language) to acknowledge the judgment that any morally sensitive person must make. In the course of such judgments Marx often passes bitter sarcasm on the moral judgments conventionally visited by governments and owners of capital on the circumstances in question. Here is an example from Chapter 15 of *Capital I*:

Before the labour of women and children under 10 years old was forbidden in mines [in England], the capitalists considered the employment of naked women and girls, often in company with men, so far sanctioned by their moral code, and especially by their ledgers, that it was only after the passing of the Act that they had recourse to machinery. The Yankees have invented a stone-breaking machine. The English do not make use of it because the 'wretch' [i.e., agricultural labourer] who does this work gets paid for such a small portion of his labour that machinery would increase the cost of production to the capitalist. In England women are still occasionally used instead of horses for hauling barges, because the labour required to produce horses and machines is an accurately known quantity, while that required to maintain the women of the surplus population is beneath all calculation. Hence we nowhere find a more shameless squandering of human labour-power for despicable purposes than in England, the land of machinery. (5167)

In more than one place Marx expressly refers, in condemning capitalist industrial production, to the "moral degradation which arises out of the exploitation by capitalism of the labour of women and children" (522). He is equally vehement in his condemnation of "the intellectual degeneration artificially produced by transforming immature human beings into mere machines for the production of surplus-value (and there is a very clear distinction between this and the state of natural ignorance in which the mind lies fallow without losing its capacity for development, its natural fertility)" (522–3). Throughout his discussion of the conditions of labouring in England, Marx's appeal to moral considerations is transparent:

> The cheapening of labour-power, by sheer abuse of the labour of women and children, by sheer robbery of every normal condition needed for working and living, and by the sheer brutality of over-work and night-work, finally comes up against certain insuperable natural obstacles. (599)
>
> Accumulation of wealth at one pole is, therefore, at the same time accumulation of misery, the torment of labour, slavery, ignorance, brutalization and moral degradation at the opposite pole, i.e., on the side of the class that produces its own product as capital. (799)

Before leaving the subject of morality, it is appropriate to note a further piece of evidence (additional to what was given earlier in Chapter Two) establishing that Marx assigns a causal role to moral facts. In the course of discussing English agriculture, Marx, in a footnote to page 836 of *Capital I*, remarks:

> The English agricultural labourer receives only a quarter as much milk and half as much bread, as the Irish. Arthur Young already noticed the better nourishment of the latter when making his 'tour through Ireland' at the beginning of this century. The reason is simply this, that the poor Irish [capitalist] farmer is incomparably more humane than the rich English.

In fact, Arthur Young's tours of Ireland were undertaken in the late 1770s. But the theoretical importance of this (by no means isolated) passage is obvious.

The issue of morality, then, exhibits further ways in which readers of Marx have practiced upon his writings mistake. These, joining with other errors (especially those regarding history), have contributed to widespread pre-conceptions of Marx's thought that have kept some persons from reading him and disposed others to read him wrongly. This is regrettable, since Marx's writings put many good questions and often propose suggestive answers.

2

Marx is widely known to have described himself as a 'materialist'. Yet there has been persistent misunderstanding of why this description is appropriately applied to him. The key to the description lies in Marx's analysis of oppression and property.

As Marx himself acknowledged, his analysis is indebted to Ludwig Feuerbach. Feuerbach, in his most famous remark, asserted that "man is what he eats". This remark affirms the *materiality* of human beings—that we not only are material beings ourselves, but that material objects are our *life*, in the basic and straightforward sense that the food in the garden or on the counter-top or in the cupboard is my life, just in that, except I take it in, *I cease to be*. Hence the neediness of human beings for access to the stuffs and products of the material world. Hence too their vulnerability to coercion, since whoever has power over what human beings need in order to eat (say), has power over them, who "are" what they eat, in the sense indicated.

Marx was not alone in seeing that the dependence of human beings on material means of subsistence confers power on whoever owns or controls the means, process and products of producing in a society. What especially distinguishes his work is his attempt to think out fully the implications of this fact for all the various aspects of human life. (Thus the ambitious youthful prospectus quoted in Chapter 3.) One of Marx's earliest essays explores the implications of the fact that lack of money is lack of freedom in societies with money economies and effectively enforced property rights. In such societies, what persons lack the money to do, they are not free to do, whatever the political or legal rhetoric of the community. Marx never expressly states the matter in this way. But this is what he understood, and sought (not always clearly) to urge the importance of.[3]

Marx also understood that property rights are historical constructions, which are everywhere liable to be interpreted according to the interests of those who advance and enforce them, however general the language in which these rights-claims may be framed. This insight, together with the above fact about money, is the burden of the two early essays jointly titled *On The Jewish Question*, in which Marx argues that many of the so-called 'rights of man' of France and the United States are, in fact, the rights asserted by owners of capitalist property against one another, the poor, and the 'sovereign' state. Marx claims that the 'free citizen' of each of these states is, in reality, the owner of capitalist property, who alone is free of the constraints imposed by lack of money and subjection to oppressive and insecure conditions of work.

In these two early essays Marx also shows a discerning appreciation of the effects of economic and political arrangements on human culture and sensibility. The two essays have been accused by a number of commentators of being anti-semitic. But this judgment neglects their basic point. Throughout the essays, Marx exploits the ambiguity of the word '*Judentum*', which at that time in the several states comprising 'Germany' could be used to mean either 'Jewry' or 'commerce'. The Jews and commerce were linked together in the German language for a reason that is basic to Marx's argument. That argument is that the language of 'citizenship', 'rights', and 'political emancipation' ignores the material reality of German life. The Jews in Germany were, more than any other group, visibly forced to seek security through money, because German citizenship and its protections and opportunities (such as these were) were denied them. But this vaunted citizenship, Marx argues, is no security to the majority of non-Jews either. In German society, the real, actual social relationships of persons one to another are governed by their economic relations and transactions—what Marx (following Hegel) terms their relations in 'civil society'. The so-called 'rights of citizenship' are in fact simply these economic claims and relations enshrined in political constitutions guaranteeing the upholding of these economic relationships and powers. This is the reason why Marx in the second of the two essays speaks of all Germans as Jews. He means that all Germans, whether Jew or Christian, are in fact in the condition of Jews, in that they are forced to practice "Judaism"—"huckstering"—in order to sustain and reproduce their life. It is in this sense that Marx asserts that "the practical [i.e., real, living, breathing, needing] Christian" (who "from the beginning was the theorizing Jew") "has become a Jew again". This, too, is the sense in which Marx speaks of "the Jewish narrowness of [German] society". It is narrow in that virtually every aspect of the lives of each person is shaped and constrained (and so preoccupied) by the possession or lack of money.

Marx's insight into the connection of economic circumstances to cultural and psychological life is evident throughout his writings. Here is one further example from *Capital I*. Marx has been discussing child labour, and he quotes from the concluding report of the Children's Employment Commission in England, published in 1866, this statement: "It is, unhappily, to a painful degree apparent throughout the whole of the evidence, that against no persons do the children of both sexes so much require protection as against their parents. . . . Parents must not possess the absolute power of making their children mere machines to earn so much wage. . ." (620. Marx then comments:

> It was not however the misuse of parental power that created the direct or indirect exploitation of immature labour-powers by capital, but rather the opposite, i.e., the capitalist mode of exploitation, by sweeping away the economic foundation which corresponded to parental power, made the use of parental power into its misuse. (620)

Throughout his detailed, empirically grounded observations upon specific connections between the economy of a society and features of its culture, Marx repudiates any simple, one-way determination thesis. He is sensitive to the interactive relation between economic circumstances and cultural and psychological states. At the same time, he is continually aware of the universally recognized fact that certain minimal conditions are necessary for human beings to achieve not only health but a basic moral sensitivity and humanity toward one another. To give just one example, in Chapter 25 Marx quotes the following sentences from the 1866 British *Eighth Report on Public Health*, prepared by a Dr. Hunter.

> 'There can be little doubt that the great cause of the continuance and spread of the typhus has been the over-crowding of human beings, and the uncleanliness of their dwellings. The rooms, in which labourers in many cases live, are situated in confined and unwholesome yards or courts, and for space, light, air, and cleanliness, are models of insufficiency and insalubrity, and a disgrace to any civilized community; in them, men, women, and children lie at night huddled together; and as regards the men, the night-shift succeed the day shift, and the dayshift the night-shift, in unbroken series for some time together, the beds having scarcely time to cool; the whole house badly supplied with water and worse with privies; dirty, unventilated, and pestiferous.' The price per week of such lodgings ranges from 8d to 3s. 'The town of Newcastle-on-Tyne,' says Dr. Hunter, 'contains a sample of the finest tribe of our countrymen, often sunk by external circumstances of house and street into an almost savage degradation.' (816)

3

Marx is famous for his opposition to religion. Yet, here too, both the promise and the mistake in his position are often overlooked. The gist of Marx's position (which is greatly indebted to Hegel and Feuerbach) is that religion is "the *fantastic* realization of the human being inasmuch as the human being possesses no true reality".[4] The governing idea is that intolerable conditions of human existence dispose human beings to (literally) make a sense of human life that renders tolerable their present existence—usually by positing some future condition in which all the wants and sorrows of present existence will be replaced by a perfect answering of human needs and aspirations. Religion, in other words, is one more part of the economy of human need satisfaction.

This is a deeply suggestive idea, that deserves extensive application to religious (and other) forms of life and belief to determine how far it is true and illuminating of them.

However (as already remarked in an earlier chapter), it is a mistake to suppose that what truth there is to this idea alone shows religious beliefs to be false. The fact (supposing it is a fact) that religious beliefs are arrived at under the press of painful and despairing circumstances does not therefore establish that they are false, any more than the fact that theories about the causes and cures of diseases are ordinarily arrived at under the press of these diseases' ravages therefore makes those theories false.

A similar mistake is frequently made regarding Marx's ideas about political institutions and practices. Marx obviously writes about political phenomena from a deeply engaged position. This is often held (unannounced) to warrant scepticism about his analysis of politics, on the grounds that any analysis that is morally charged must be a piece of political apology, not a truth-functional description. The limpness of this objection when baldy stated is no bar to its operating upon persons' judgments. A cruder, but still influential, error is the supposition that because brutal things have been done by persons describing themselves as 'Marxists', the political writings of Marx cannot deserve study.

In fact, Marx's basic thesis regarding politics is a corollary of his insights into property and oppression. Effective political action by members of capitalist industrial societies requires at the very least money (or direct command of manpower) and knowledge. Those who possess significant amounts of the first can more effectively pursue their political purposes through electoral and governmental arrangements whose personnel depend on them for fiscal and other kinds of cooperation and support (including continued investment). At the same time, these persons are better able to acquire the knowledge they need and to influence the kind and extent of 'information' available to the rest of the society. In short, on Marx's view, those who dominate production are strategically placed to dominate politically, and often do dominate politically, so as to be better assured of continuing to dominate production.

This is a plausible and, in several respects, well-substantiated position regarding political processes and structures whose claim on the attention of political inquiry has been incisively argued by Noam Chomsky and Edward Herman, Joshua Cohen and Joel Rogers, Richard Miller, and others.[5] The position explains Marx's lifetime commitment to replacing non-democratic with democratic institutional arrangements, including the instituting of broad democratic control over economic investment decisions as necessary to achieve political and social equality among the members of large-scale industrial societies. The position also explains Marx's concern throughout his writings to expose economic arrangements that make achievement of genuine community of feeling and regard between human beings difficult or impossible. It was Marx's judgment always that the creation of a humane society inescapably involved genuine community between human beings.

4

Finally we have already seen in the previous chapter Marx's prescient remarks in *Capital* about the ecological hazards of capitalist production. We have also seen there passages which reveal Marx's insight into the technologically revolutionary momentum of capitalism, and its probable human consequences. I refer to such passages as:

> Modern industry never views or treats the existing form of a production process as the definitive one. Its technical basis is therefore revolutionary, whereas all earlier modes of production were essentially conservative. By means of machinery, chemical processes and other methods it is continually transforming not only the technical basis of production but also the functions of the worker and the social combinations of the labour process. At the same time, it thereby also revolutionizes the division of labour within society, and incessantly throws masses of capital and of workers from one branch of production to another. (617)

Note how compellingly apt Marx's words are of the *computer* and *robotic* applications of the last few decades in industry, and distribution ("just-in-time ordering", etc.), *and* in capitalist ownership and control (multi-national enterprises commanding wealth exceeding many United Nations' members, and exhibiting no loyalties whatever to the human communities whose generations of labour and intelligence produced that wealth).

Marx could not have anticipated that *these* specific late-capitalist developments would be among the factors that may conceivably yet show capitalism to be unviable. But the prescience of his recognition of the *kind* of developments capitalism was prone to is undeniable.

5

It has not been my purpose in this concluding chapter to treat in detail any of the above themes in Marx's writings, but only to indicate in outline their content and to give the reader reason to judge that previous commentary or report ought not to be relied upon.

Rather, a fresh reading, or re-reading, ought to begin. At the same time, neither is it my purpose (as I hope the previous four chapters make clear) to suggest that Marx's writings contain no mistake. I am claiming that Marx's writings deserve study uncontaminated by the kinds of error identified in this book. But no one who takes those writings up to study them must expect to find no error in them.

Indeed, the opening pages of *Capital I*, which address the basic category of a 'commodity', contain mistakes of an elementary kind. In these pages Marx purports to deduce the famous 'labour theory of value'. He does so by asking us to consider two commodities, iron and corn, which exchange in different quantities one for the other; "for instance 1 quarter of corn = x cwt [hundred weight] of iron" (127). Marx then asks what this equation signifies, and replies: "It signifies that a common element of identical magnitude exists in two different things, in one quarter of corn and similarly in x cwt of iron" (127). He then goes on to invite us to conclude that this common element can only be the iron and corn's "being products of labour" (128). There are two errors observable in this reasoning. The first is the unwarranted conclusion that the explanation of the exchange equivalence must lie in some "*common element*" that "exists in" each of the two different things. Marx thinks not of some property or relation common to both commodities that explains their exchange equivalence, such as a common relation of the commodities' respective qualities to something outside them (e.g, the various needs or purposes of human beings). Marx thinks of something "in" each that is the explanation of the exchange equivalence. This sets him up for the second error, which is what he fixes upon as this common element: "homogeneous human labour" that is "accumulated" or "congealed" in each (128). Marx rejects, as explanation of the equivalence, utility to human beings.

This utility has, ordinarily, a certain cost to produce (which cost being borne by human beings is a register of that utility). This cost can be 'paid' either by human beings directly employing resources, energy, and time to produce a product having this utility, or by their exchanging other useful things to obtain such a product. In such a transaction, the different quantities in which two commodities exchange is at least partly a function of their different utilities to human beings. Yet Marx resolutely refuses to accord "use value" (as he calls it) any part in the explanation, on the grounds that it is not "abstract" enough to account for exchange values (127). Later, however (as we have seen), he frequently takes account of utilities and their accompanying demand functions.

These errors of Marx in the early pages of *Capital I* are, as I have said, elementary, and the kind a first year university student can be brought to appreciate and avoid. But they are no register of the worth of what follows them. And even in the course of committing them Marx raises, however confusedly, two basic questions concerning economic transactions: what constitutes 'producing' a product, and according to what standard are producers to be rewarded in market transactions?

To conclude, the verdict on Marx's contribution to social understanding is still to be reached, in my judgment. In reaching it, readers of Marx must avoid the kinds of error identified in this book. In particular, they must look to Marx's practice, not his pronouncements. This holds, of course, for any other inquirer, and for any kind of inquiry. When taking up to appraise it any offering in any subject, we must attend not to the theorist, but the theory; not the singer, but the song.

Notes

CHAPTER ONE

1. G.A. Cohen, *Karl Marx's Theory of History. A Defence* (Princeton: Princeton University Press, 1978; *History, Labour, and Freedom: Themes From Marx* (Oxford: Clarendon Press, 1988). Hereafter each will in most instances be cited in parentheses in the text, initials first (*KMTH, HLF*), followed by the page number.
2. *KMTH* 255, 262–3, 269–71, 285–89.
3. John Ostrom, "Bird Flight: how did it begin?" *American Scientist*, Vol. 67, 1979, 46–56.
4. Stephen Jay Gould, *The Panda's Thumb* (New York: W.W. Norton & Company, 1982) 275–6.
5. Richard C. Lewontin, "Testing the Theory of Natural Selection", *Nature*, 1972, 182.
6. *HLF* 23, 90–1; *KMTH* 159. See also *KMTH* 144 and *HLF* 122–3.
7. Robert C. Tucker (ed.), *The Marx-Engels Reader*, Second Edition (New York: W.W. Norton & Company, 1978) 136. Other writings of Marx quoted from this collection will hereafter be cited: Tucker, *MER*, followed by the page number.
8. Tucker, *MER* 137.

CHAPTER TWO

1. G.F.W. Hegel, *Philosophy of Right*, transl. T.M. Knox (Oxford: Clarendon Press, 1952) 235–6. (Addition 24 to Paragraph 41.)
2. Tucker, *MER* 144.
3. Ibid., 218.
4. David S. Landes, *Revolution in Time: Clocks and the Making of the Modern World* (Cambridge, Mass.: Harvard University Press, 1983).

5. Jean-Jacques Rousseau, *Discourse on the Origin of Inequality*, translated by Donald A. Cress (Indianapolis: Hackett Publishing Company, 1983) 140.

6. David S. Landes, *The Unbound Prometheus: Technological Change and Industrial Development in Western Europe from 1750 to the Present* (Cambridge: Cambridge University Press, 1969). All references are to the 1988 sixteenth (papercover) printing.

7. G. E. von Grunebaum, *Islam: Essays in the Nature and Growth of a Cultural Tradition* (London, 1961) quoted by Landes at 28–9.

8. Tucker, *MER* 53.

CHAPTER THREE

1. Tucker, *MER* 67.
2. Ibid., 84–5.
3. Ibid., 34.
4. Afterword to the Second (German) Edition of *Capital*, Volume One, translated by Ben Fowkes (New York: Vintage Books, 1977)100–101. Further references to this work will be given by page number in parentheses following a quotation.
5. All quotations from this work are from first and last sections of the essay, reproduced in Tucker, *MER* 595–617.
6. Tucker *MER* 471.
7. "The British Rule in India" (10 June 1853) and "The Future Results of British Rule in India" (22 July 1853), in Tucker *MER* 653–8, 659–64.
8. "Contribution to the Critique of Hegel's *Philosophy of Right*: Introduction", in Tucker *MER* 53–65.
9. Stephen Jay Gould, *Wonderful Life: The Burgess Shale and the Nature of History* (New York: W. W. Norton & Company, 1989).

CHAPTER FOUR

1. *Selected Correspondence*, ed. S.W. Ryazanskaya (Moscow: Progress Publishers, 1969) 293–4.
2. Tucker, *MER* 483.
3. Ibid., 483.
4. Ibid., 172.

CHAPTER FIVE

1. Allen Wood, "The Marxian Critique of Justice", *Philosophy and Public Affairs* Volume 1, 1972; Richard W. Miller, *Analyzing Marx. Morality, Power and History* (Princeton: Princeton University Press, 1984), Chapters One and Two.

2. For the arguments establishing this, see Rodger Beehler, *Moral Life* (Oxford: Basil Blackwell, 1978; Totowa, NJ: Rowman and Littlefield, 1978), especially chapters I-IV.

3. See further Rodger Beehler, " For One Concept of Liberty", *Journal of Applied Philosophy*, Vol 8, No 1, 1991, 27–43, in which the conceptions of liberty of Isaiah Berlin, Charles Taylor, and others are shown to be wanting.

4. Tucker *MER* 54.

5. Noam Chomsky and Edward Herman, *Political Economy of Human Rights*, Two Volumes (Montreal: Black Rose Books, 1979) and *Manufacturing Consent* (New York: Pantheon Books, 1988); Joshua Cohen and Joel Rogers, *On Democracy* (New York: Penguin Books, 1983); Richard W. Miller, *Analyzing Marx* (Princeton: Princeton University Press, 1984.)

www.ingramcontent.com/pod-product-compliance
Lightning Source LLC
Chambersburg PA
CBHW021408290426
44108CB00010B/440